The Shapes of Structure

HEATHER MARTIENSSEN

Oxford University Press

LONDON OXFORD NEW YORK
GLASGOW TORONTO MELBOURNE WELLINGTON
CAPE TOWN IBADAN NAIROBI DAR ES SALAAM LUSAKA ADDIS ABABA
DELHI BOMBAY CALCUTTA MADRAS KARACHI LAHORE DACCA
KUALA LUMPUR SINGAPORE HONG KONG TOKYO

© *Oxford University Press 1976*

First published in the Oxford Paperbacks
University Series 1976 and simultaneously
in a cloth bound edition.

Martienssen, Heather
  The shapes of structure.
  Bibl.—Index.
  ISBN 0-19-217646-3
  ISBN 0-19-289075-1 Pbk.
  1. Title
  721'.09   NA 2750
  Architectural design—History

*Filmset in 'Monophoto' Ehrhardt 10 on 12 pt. by
Richard Clay (The Chaucer Press), Ltd., Bungay, Suffolk
and printed in Great Britain by
Fletcher & Son Ltd., Norwich*

The Shapes of Structure

Oxford University Press

LONDON · OXFORD · NEW YORK

197

REX
In memory

Acknowledgements

My thanks go to members of the Departments of Fine Arts and Art History of the University of the Witwatersrand, Johannesburg for their sympathy and patience while I was writing this book, and for their kindness in undertaking extra tasks so that I could have the time to finish it; I am deeply indebted to Architect Monte Bryer and Art Historian Elizabeth Rankin for reading the first draft and giving me the benefit of their special knowledge; I am indebted too to Moyra Oldham for typing the manuscript at all its stages and helping me in so many ways; and finally I must thank the Senate of the University for voting me financial assistance towards the illustrations.

It has been a pleasure to work with Carol Buckroyd of the Oxford University Press and her team, and the smoothing of so many rough edges is entirely due to her unflagging wit and alertness.

Part of the section on the Aesthetic of the Plan first appeared in the British Journal of Aesthetics, Autumn 1974.

Heather Martienssen
London, January 1976

Contents

Illustrations

The marginal references in the text are to the illustrations: to the number of the illustration as in the list above or, where preceded by *p*, to the page on which an un-numbered illustration appears.

Introduction: In Praise of Precedence

'Commodity, firmness, and delight'—so Sir Henry Wootton rendered Vitruvius's requirement for all buildings, *'Firmitas, Utilitas, Venustas'*.[1] Vitruvius lived during the reign of Augustus, and there may have been earlier writers on architecture. His precept may have been a common one. But for us he was the first, and although it is the fashion to belittle his style and smile at the content of his *Ten Books*,[2] this much-quoted and variously translated injunction would alone entitle him to our very great regard.

Vitruvius has had as little praise and as much emulation at least in his writing as any architect, and it may be noted that some of the best as well as some of the worst books on architecture have been written by architects. The best justify and explain the author's own work, and analyse from this creative viewpoint the environment of historic and modern architecture to which he means to belong. The worst provide rules for unsubstantiated standards of excellence, and a view of history which is either intolerably smug or unforgivably faulty. Architects are not often scholars, and it is a peculiar obstinacy that even today leads, in some schools of architecture, to the teaching of architectural history by architects, and not by architectural historians. The professional architect suspects the scholar of one knows not what. Certainly of a wrong bias in his approach to history, or perhaps to the quality of architecture. Probably this has arisen because historic architecture was originally shown as examples for young architects to follow, and only an architect who was in practice himself would be able properly to counsel and instruct. Architectural pedagogues are now belatedly realizing that historic styles are no longer useful for emulation and, as few architects are interested in old buildings, there has been a noticeable drop in enthusiasm over the last few decades for the teaching of the history of architecture to architectural students.

Architectural historians continue to produce brilliant virtuoso exercises, even if, as we begin to suspect, they are now read only by other architectural historians. The taking in of each other's washing is not yet as bad as it was in the eighteenth century, when two rival authors sometimes dipped so profusely into each other's works that by the second or third editions it was no longer possible to remember who had got in first. It did not really matter anyway. It had all probably started with an English version of Palladio or Alberti, who as we all know had the pattern from Vitruvius in the first place. Nothing half so brilliant as Reynolds's *Discourses* came from an architect for the summing up of the classical intention. His contemporary, Sir William Chambers, made an attempt (almost immediately abandoned) to emulate him by producing 'discourses' on architecture. Something of what he was preparing for these appeared in his *Treatise on Civil Architecture*, in which he wrote:

> No subject hath been more amply treated of than Architecture, nor any by persons more capable; in so much that few things remain either to be discovered or improved, every branch of the Art having been maturely considered, and brought very near the utmost degree of certainty of which it is capable.[3]

This almost incredible statement is itself a revelation of the position architecture had got itself into even before the end of the eighteenth century. In a sense Chambers was right. The architecture of his world had reached the end after three hundred years of fluency and, as we shall try to show, it was almost the fade-out of the architect as such, at least in the guise in which he had presented himself for so long.

The architect tends to write about practical things, and since the historian is fastidious about committing himself to any but stylistic assessments, literature on the philosophy and 'aesthetic' of architecture is less profuse by far than that in the field of painting. So-called 'theory' of architecture tends to be the theoretical side of design and construction, whether didactic or analytic. Even where writers expound richly on the nature of art, this can rarely be applied directly to architecture, especially in the realm of feeling. Even the conception of architecture as the 'mother' of the arts implies the provision of a zone of nutrition and protection, and not an archetype. In spite of this, the question of architecture's being an art has never been seriously raised. It is assumed (and the assumption is not here challenged) that the Parthenon 'must' be a work of art and therefore other buildings may be works of art. Though this can be side-stepped by claiming that the Greek temple is monumental sculpture and not architecture at all, we cannot sustain this sort of evasion throughout history. What about Chartres, and many other buildings?

10, 23

Perhaps it was easier to equate architecture with the other arts when elegance and even beauty in the classical or romantic sense were the norm. The Greek temple 'goes with' the Kouros, Amiens with its own portal carvings, the Venetian Palazzo with Carpaccio, Osterley Park with Gainsborough. We can also parallel Le Corbusier and Mies van der Rohe with their contemporaries and collaborators like Ozenfant, Léger, and the creators of de Stijl. But who else with whom? Even Picasso, let alone other artists since the forties and fifties, is not easily interpreted in architecture. Man moves in multi-directional space, but always relates himself to the horizontal and vertical. The lines of a plan may depart from formal relations, but in so far as they imply enclosing verticals they have to offer their tenant a minimal confidence. The definitive names of the

40, p134

parts of a building, floors, walls, roofs, doors, windows, restrict the architect to a certain kind of performance. He cannot, as the sculptor may, project towards his spectator pure fashioning in an expressive or formal field. Not only this, but for the mechanical functioning of his movable units (doors, windows, lifts) as well as for the equilibrium of his tenant referred to above, he will always need to use rectilinear shapes as a major, visual character in his work, however unfashionable they may become in the other arts, and whether or not organic or 'free' forms are used in the design.

This control of architecture by its own functional necessity may give to its development a certain autonomy. While the function and structural methods remain fairly stationary, style is merely fashion. Houses were built and used in much the same way from the early eighteenth century until the twentieth. Style was a matter of detail and proportional relations, and in England for example moved easily through Georgian, Regency, Victorian, and Edwardian without any fundamental change. When iron was admitted into the structural vocabulary it became a part of the style, and the late nineteenth-century domestic buildings put out a show of frilly cast-iron petticoats. The far-reaching effects which the new material was to have hardly showed in this flippancy, but the new architecture was at the same time emerging in railway stations and viaducts, in harbours and market halls.

It is easy for us to see now that this 'tough' architecture was the real stuff of the nineteenth century, but it is not so easy to bring this awareness forward into our own world. To follow the course of architecture emerging from its old skin towards renewed assertion, it is necessary for us to jettison much of the clutter that comes from the slow by-products of advance tempered by nostalgia. The rejection of course is almost wholly figurative: one does not want to destroy all old buildings, only the obsolete. It should be realized here that a proper work of architecture never becomes obsolete. If it has efficiently served a purpose, it will always be efficient *for that purpose*. It is purposes that are obsolescent, not works of art. That is why we preserve fine old buildings.

In any case if the forms of architecture resulted, as some have wished to believe, entirely from function, all buildings serving similar functions would appear the same, but in fact there are few building types whose functional intention has been so despotic as to impose an invariable shape. Certainly plans will group themselves according to the purposes to be served, but the form of a building is far more likely to reflect the materials and structural methods, not to say the taste, of its day, than the uses to which it may be put. Certain austerities in advanced taste earlier in this century often provoked the comment that a commercial block looked 'like a factory', a hotel 'like a hospital', a house 'like a box'. Now this last comment might be considered the most valid, for a box has a basic formal economy that can be applied to a larger structural programme, whereas there is no logical meaning in likening one building type to another, especially when they do serve similar purposes. All through history man-made objects seem to have fallen into forms or groups of forms suitable to their purpose, and one kind of analysis of structures can liken them to these.

This kind of analogy in fact, if not pushed ridiculously far can help especially in an attempt to define what one might consider the temperament of a building. What is delightful to contemplation is so largely because of association, recognized or tacit, and that association in buildings may well lie in realms other than the directly utilitarian. Once the demands of *utilitas* (perhaps quite simple) have been catered for, the architect's way is open to a variety of alternative methods of providing an adequate *firmitas* and a *venustas* appropriate to his day. How various this may be the history of architecture shows, but it shows also that certain shapes and attitudes to the provision of space, enclosed or partly so, will tend to provoke similar responses and associations which will be only partly modified according to materials and constructional methods used. The equipment of the architect therefore, like the equipment of all artists, has not changed so completely as might be superficially supposed. The provision of space and mass, light, shade, and colour may have become available by different means, but have always been available within the imaginative range exercised by any generation, and within its own sphere of operation.

The exercise of apprehending architecture involves awareness of a character emerging from the marshalling of the materials used towards ends complex in their intention, and thus seldom if ever grasped in their totality. For those who want to evade the results of a programmatic approach, there may be some consolation in the fact that even the programmatic is ultimately determined by an organic reaction to means at hand, and to the essential fertility and resilience of the designer's mind.

The architectural profession has always included a number of men of ability who put out elegant buildings, adequate for their purpose, and using structural and mechanical knowledge of their day. This I have called 'anonymous' architecture. But important architecture will go further than this. It will push forward the resources of its day. The necessity of this advance may not be set aside by the querulous protest that innovation is not necessary to art. In significant art the imaginative range is always extended; in architecture the structural equipment is so fundamental to its constitution that designing flexes with its every extension. This does not mean that every fine building represents a major breakthrough; most good architecture is, rather, an affirmation of what is valid in its day. Affirmation is not the same as repetition. Nor is a major break-

through necessarily attributable to a single building or a single architect. The
stone temple in Greece was a breakthrough into awareness of possible technical   10, 23
precision and visual *symmetria*. The individual temples stand as affirmation of
that awareness, of what is becoming known. Final knowledge does not appear in
art: sophistication is not the perfection of innocence. We find the same sort of
affirmation in the structural flowering of the French cathedrals. The breakthrough is nowhere singly demonstrated. But after the collective affirmation of
the thirteenth century the great moment is past. Nothing is possible after
Amiens. All the rest is reaffirmation, which is not the same as affirmation.   40, p134

The Eiffel Tower is a single, if not singular, affirmatory building of the   41
nineteenth century which, while purporting to be merely a demonstration of
structural virtuosity, remains a great work of art. The phenomenon emphasizes
the structural adventure of so-called civil engineering as an important division
of architecture. In the years of the building of the Eiffel Tower (1887 to 1889)
Impressionist painting was reaching its last phase of structural dissolution and
surface integration. The last Impressionist exhibition was held in 1886, but the
central group of painters including Monet and Renoir carried on to see the style
to its logical conclusion. Seurat had reached the apex of Pointillism, a fragmen-
tation of the picture surface, with his *Grande-Jatte* of 1886, and Monet was to
paint in 1894 his series of Rouen Cathedral. Van Gogh had moved south from
Paris to begin his mature but restless spate of landscape and still-life. The short
and violent Fauve years were still to come. Cézanne and Gauguin had already
turned to that orderly assemblage which would become so soon after Fauvism
the Cubist manner, regarded almost from its beginnings as seminal for the
twentieth century, as the structural adventures were themselves to prove. But
between 1851 (which was the year of the Crystal Palace and King's Cross
Station) and the Frank Lloyd Wright houses of the turn of the century, there
were few signs that civic and domestic architecture were facing contemporary
problems with any kind of contemporary conviction. Even in apartment houses
and other multi-storeyed buildings on the Continent and in America, though one
finds much of historical significance, they are rare examples which evoke that
sense of wonder and exaltation we are visited with when confronting what we
recognize as art. This is the fifty years during which Jacob in the guise of the
engineer slowly took on Esau's birthright, leaving his elder brother to discover
that the mess of pottage, so dearly bought, was not even to remain palatable.

It was Le Corbusier's great gift to recognize that architecture was not just the
trimming on the cake; the austere temper of his immediate followers was inevitably the only antidote to the lazy-minded thinking of the generations before
him, and perhaps it will not have proved too late for architecture to recover
its lost heritage. We are, however, in the situation today of requiring in our

environment structures which the architect in his old capacity is no longer able to provide. Only the engineer seems equipped for the new imaginative calculations, and he is doubly ready now after more than a century of waiting upon the architect's petulant prettiness. Engineers, sometimes but not irrevocably in partnership with architects, are providing a new language of structure.

I
The Art of Building

Architecture as Art

The assertion that architecture is an art has been put forward so often and with so many justifications that it arouses in itself an interest: not whether architecture is or is not an art but why the justifications should be necessary. The ready explanation may well be that *bad* building is not architecture, and therefore not art, but then neither is bad painting nor bad sculpture art, and no one has ever felt the need to show that they are. We all know that architecture differs from sculpture and painting in that it is fundamentally utilitarian. First it functions as some sort of protection, for which it must be structured, and the question of its managing to achieve any status as a work of art arises from the way this structuring is done. This is not a situation that parallels itself in any of the other arts, except those which might be considered as extensions to architecture itself, such as furniture, glass or china, silverware and fabric, for even if we consider function in painting and sculpture (such as portraiture) or literature (such as narrative or description) these functions are themselves part of the world of imagination and do not set up the ideological dichotomies so often encountered in building.* If we may reduce the situation to a simple suggestion, it is that a building may adequately fulfil its purpose while being aesthetically negligible while a painting or poem may not, for if it is not aesthetically acceptable it has not fulfilled its purpose.

Even the term 'art' has to be approached with caution today. Ever since Herbert Read and his generation so convincingly demonstrated that Art and Beauty were not interchangeable terms, and that a work of art was 'often a thing of no beauty', it has become impossible for us to claim that anything was a work of art because it was agreed to be beautiful, or conversely that we should look for demonstrable beauty to show that a thing was a work of art.

The possibility of beauty, even in the classical sense, has never been denied. Although there may be no general agreement on its constituents, it is assumed to be easily found in nature, the animal and human world and (we may suppose) simple objects. It is only in the world of art that we must tread cautiously because it has been shown that the way in which a work of art may move us is quite different from the casual grace of nature, that it may be formidable, frightening, disturbing, and yet lead to that satisfaction and acceptance that we associate with the apprehension of the emotionally significant. The artist may approach us through arrangements that could be regarded as beautiful, and in other generations this has bountifully happened. Even recently 'Op' artists have

---

* Even didactic literature, which would include sermons and other kinds of persuasion, draws its strength more from its presentation than its logic, which in any case involves a handling of human imagination.

made use of patterns and shapes that were delightful in a simple way. But art of more depth has found this increasingly difficult. To reach the satiated, heavily protected sensibilities of contemporary viewers the art attack has sometimes become very violent indeed.

Now with this almost insoluble problem of identification, classification, and assessment of the arts generally today (with the impossibility, for example, of isolating them in the traditional categories of 'painting' or 'sculpture'), how do we approach the task of setting up any sort of critical equipment for the apprehension of architecture? Its utilitarian rôle led to the establishment of the whole concept of 'functionalism', which meant simply, not that the building would necessarily function better, but that it was to look as if it did. This could lead in fact to so many evasions that the building did not function at all. (Functionalism was never a term popular with architects themselves.) Out of 'functional' aesthetics came those that included 'Brutalism', which implied no concealment of actuality, a difficult ideal in complex planning and equipment.* In some quarters today an anarchy has arisen in which young architects are suspicious of almost *all* tradition.

The individually brilliant perception of a way of approach is not necessarily going to provide a general direction for architects. The greatest single genius of the century has been Le Corbusier. Now at last universally accepted, the principles on which he proceeded rather than his actual works, which were proper to his generation, may have far-reaching effects upon those who can interpret them as a way of defining the rôle of architecture, and particularly the aesthetic implications of that rôle, in environmental determination on a world scale.

There will always be one complication to the establishment of architecture as art which does not seem to have been adequately considered in the assessment of individual buildings and groups of buildings, and that is the presence of people. The disorder of casual human usage is surely a visual factor endemic to any building, and must be considered in visual assessment as it is in practical designing. Architects are usually concerned to have their work seen (and certainly photographed) empty, except for furniture and fittings selected by them for the purpose. This promotes an unreal situation in which we regard the work almost as we would a piece of sculpture, in itself a final statement. A building cannot be complete without its tenants, as a stage set, however brilliantly painted, is not complete without its actors. (And this has been the weakness in many stage sets and especially backdrops designed by great artists.) A building, emptied in the natural course of the day's programme, is *locked up*, a symbolic as well as a practical gesture, signifying that it is excluded for a while from human experience of it, except for its face, looking silently, darkly, but perhaps

* The New Brutalism emanated in 1954 from English architects Peter and Alison Smithson.

significantly over its appointed place in the townscape. If it is especially fine or significant it may even be floodlit, as if to emphasize its continuity in the life of that environment.

(Chairs can never be works of art, because they are always incomplete, standing about waiting for occupants.)*

It may well be that mankind has unconsciously paid greatest tribute to works that are complete without its presence. The Greek temple, housing the cult-image for which it was built, is complete. So is the pyramid over the buried Pharaoh, and the crypt of the saint with its few ritual guardians. Only to a slightly lesser degree is the great church complete without a full congregation. Built for a mystic Occupation it accepts with equal indifference a solitary acolyte or verger attending to the lamps or a milling crowd of pilgrims. By night, its doors perhaps closed, its outward splendours continue to give character and even comfort to the city over which it presides. But a house needs its household, schools their children, and most particularly, theatres their actors and audiences. If they are not there we tend to evoke their presence. 'This is where they sat,' we say looking down nostalgically into a deserted Greek theatre, and from the broken *logeion*, 'their voices carried, you know, to the highest tiers.' The viewer will often enjoy an empty place, but with awareness of a significant negation.

Can we make a new criterion for the judgement of architecture? Can we say, if the presence of the tenants for whom this building was designed, doing those things that are meant to be done here, detracts from the total visual adequacy of this building, then it cannot be a work of art in the fullest sense, but at most a seemly container waiting to fulfil its function? Let us try this out with a few buildings generally accepted as being important works of architecture. Temples, churches, and tombs have been considered above, and actual examples will easily present themselves. What about theatres? The theatre of Epidaurus is still frequently used, but in fairness it should be pictured with an audience and actors of its own time. It would surely lose nothing by coming to life with the activity for which it was designed; the philosophically or austerely minded could stand aside as the auditorium emptied after the show to brood over the wonderful vast shell resting between performances. The Roman baths and basilicas too must have been augmented and given meaning by the presence and bustle of people, the ornate vaults soaring uninterruptedly over their heads. At Versailles the now almost tawdry Hall of Mirrors was once alive and glittering

10, 23

5

p126

---

* However bedecked and contrived they may be. There is some hesitation as to whether one may regard a ritual chair as a work of art, charged as it is with emotive association. The ritual chairs of certain African rulers, or the Cathedra of St. Peter's in Rome or of Amiens forming a part of the Baroque background to the altar belong to this class.

with the costumes of courtiers and supplicants, while the great houses of the
Renaissance and subsequent centuries, gaunt today, must have been grander
and more fulfilled with their original tenants and furnishings. Perhaps the best
of all examples from a later date is the railway station, seldom deserted, except
in the small hours, but as exciting as a Monet with the coming, going, and
waiting of people and trains.* What applies to the railway station applies also to
the piazza. Even the most formal of them, like Bernini's great oval at St. Peter's
is not destroyed by enormous crowds: that is what it was built for. The piazza
and piazzetta at Venice, among the most evocative and satisfactory arrangements of squares in western Europe, are equally (but differently) enchanting,
teeming or deserted.

This is not to deny that alone-ness and emptied spaces do not evoke powerful
emotions, and perhaps the distancing from a 'real' situation does itself promote
an 'art' quality. But the aesthetic of loneliness and its accompanying sensations
should perhaps be distinguished from acceptance of an architectural complex
whole, that is definitely to say functioning. The precious (in every sense)
privilege of the scholar in analysing or experiencing the methods by which the
artist has achieved his effect is not in the first sense apprehension of the work
itself, just as reading a plan is not in the direct sense 'seeing' a building. An extension
to both the reading of plans and seeing buildings is afforded by the airview
photograph, which for this reason is one of the most important aids to experience.
The strengthened awareness of tri-dimensional mass and volume is due to the
position of the photographer which is more advantageous than any at ground level.

In the present-day world this harmony between container and contained is
not always so evident, though it can be found. The examples above do involve
contemporary crowds, but they are pedestrians. Not so happy is the sight of
traffic hurtling around the Colosseum or jamming the market squares of
country towns. Only recently the Piazza Navona in Rome has been released
from use as a parking place and has retrieved the quality of its old intention: a
place of quiet movement with the leisured play of fountains. What offend us too
are certain anachronisms: cars parked against the Strozzi Palace, or office desks
and filing cabinets visible (as Piper points out[1]) in the windows of Georgian
residences. The great clover-leaf crossing, on the other hand, comes to life with
a continuous flow of traffic, under and over, marvellously not meeting in head-
on collision, like the toy of a giant's child, and there is nothing *per se* unseemly
about a multi-storeyed parking garage.

The most difficult task for the architect (and yet surely the most ancient and

---

* The same thing cannot be said always of airports and air terminals, perhaps because this factor
has not always been fully considered.

1. St. Peter's, Rome, with Bernini's piazza beyond

fundamental?) would seem to be the provision of housing which maintains a visual adequacy while functioning according to its proper usage. It is easy for us to accept the idea of stately modes and manners in a stately eighteenth-century mansion, certainly including the chair or carriage waiting at the door. How do we proceed in designing for the habits and habiliments of the permissive Now? Cars and children's toys and even people are carefully placed out of sight before an important design is photographed. It was frequently noted during the thirties and forties by people who could not accept the 'purist' vogue led by Le Corbusier and Mies van der Rohe that living in their houses would be like living in a shop window: what about the clutter of the ordinary daily round? Presumably the patrons of La Roche and the Villa Savoye and other great Corbu houses with their modern art collections and furnishings, certainly Le Corbusier himself in his own flat, Philip Johnson in his fastidious 'Glass House' (secluded in its own plantation) have been able to live in the mode of these buildings because they were buildings designed to their mode. To transfer a wavering or indignant population from the traditional compromise of unsightly but unseen muddle and decent mediocrity into a setting devised for a different pattern of living (even if considered by the architect more convenient and delightful) is not going to work out ideally either from the sociological or visual angle.

Vernacular communities seem to go on for ever, supposedly so long as simplicity in living continues.* Urbanization is another matter and must be accepted as the condition largely obtaining. One cannot condemn future generations to obsolete quarters because their forbears would not adapt to vertical distribution and modern sanitation.

One mistake that was made in the zest for sweeping away the insalubrious palimpsests of the old domestic settings was to over-design. The built-in cupboard was accepted with enthusiasm by most housewives, but when there are also folding beds, hinged tables, rigidly disposed bookshelves, display cabinets, and even stereo brackets, not to mention of course bedside lamps and shelves, concealed lighting, wall lighting, dining recesses with fixed tables and seats, the tenant has nothing to do but move in, and though they are not officially 'furnished' quarters he has less flexibility for living than he might have if they were, and nowhere to put anything that means for him his own identity. The modern 'capsule' dwelling unit adds to this provision of built-in equipment a streamlining aesthetic that prohibits personal contribution. A recent block of these units—one cannot call them flats—in Tokyo shows a neat cylinder so mercilessly equipped with mass-necessities like tape recorders and television that all that seems to be missing is the equally neatly fitting piston. Perhaps this

* That is to say, while these groups of people, inevitably rural, continue to live in the traditional manner that has always evoked this pattern of building.

is more welcome and easier to manage in a socialist community. Perhaps private ownership is an encouragement to bad taste. No ownership may equally be an encouragement to no taste, to indifference.

During the first decades of the twentieth century when architects' attitudes to the visual character of their buildings was changing into what we might regard as the twentieth-century 'manner', the kind of shapes they wanted to encourage were very similar to those engendered in painting. This was presumably not accidental, and groups like de Stijl in Holland were fond of pointing out the similarities.[2] Painters, sculptors, and architects worked together so closely here that the horizontal and vertical lines characteristic of the paintings of Mondrian or the sculptures of van Doesburg, or the plans of the architect 34 Vantongerloo, look like each other and like the plans or models of the architects Oud or Rietveld, which in turn look like abstract* paintings and sculpture. Elevations too, even by independents like Dudok, emphasized flat roofs, horizontal windows, simple verticals. In a slightly more subtle relation formal abstracts like those of Léger and the Purists were sympathetic to the Constructivists and the architecture 53, p149 of Le Corbusier and the Bauhaus. Before this time similarities in architecture and the visual arts had been largely a question of a sympathetic ambience and mutual completion: a classical statue is made for a classical niche, a 'ruined temple' for a romantic garden, a perspective vista for a pilastered wall. But now, for perhaps the only time in history, the shapes became in some sense almost interchangeable and formal abstraction united the two spheres of design.

This was not to last very long. Almost as the world was learning to regard shape relations as the central factor in recognizing and assessing works of art the mood of the artist changed in a swing to Expressionism, and formal precision lived on chiefly in Surrealism. Twentieth-century *avant-garde* in Germany had always been Expressionist, and thus never ran exactly parallel to forward-looking architecture as promulgated by the Bauhaus. We should not look for a parallelism of this sort. The Expressionist artwork almost always looks well in a stark setting, and when architecture is thought of as a setting its appearance *vis-à-vis* the other arts becomes a matter for rather different thinking.

The difficulty in formulating an adequate aesthetic for architecture has probably lain in this double rôle we have given it; that of both monument and setting, and the attempt of architects to make it, as it were, a setting for its own monumentality. Bruno Zevi has come to grips with this in averring that architecture is concerned only with space.[3] In doing so he has rejected almost entirely the monumental or external aspects of buildings except in their rôle as backgrounds or limiting surfaces to other spaces. If we go back to the origins of

---

* 'Abstract' is used here in the sense of moving away from literal representation.

architecture to define its essential character we shall have to see it first as *shelter* and then as *container*. These are both open-ended terms, as a building has a doorway, and for the same reason. Both imply the presence of something else, the thing to be sheltered, the thing to be contained. The function may be complex or easy, but it is its *raison d'être*, and any visual satisfaction, any 'delight' that is afforded us arises surely from our apprehension of it as a functioning entity. A house, the maestro tells us, is a machine for living in. If we cannot live in it the machine does not work, and cannot be contemplated as such at all. Mere functioning however is not enough, and especially where simple, takes us nowhere at all towards visual satisfaction. We may indeed be 'delighted' to find the bathroom conveniently situated (and in fact the implications of convenience or 'commodity' may have an aesthetic aspect) but this is not quite the visual delight devised for us in great architecture. On the other hand pomp and grandeur can be the reverse of attractive where they are presented to us without convenience.

A sitting-room is a room for sitting in, a room served and sometimes presided over by the Chair. It may be a formal room, where we sit in polite conversation, or a place where we read or listen to music. When we look about us we may find pleasure in the casual grace of scattered books, or bowls of flowers translucent in sunlight. This can happen in any room. But architecture can contrive some spiritual extension by its own device: the relations of surfaces or spaces. With p149 so-called 'free' planning we may not have a sitting-room, but only a sitting zone, from which we experience the totality and variousness of the whole space at our disposal, and act and react visually to the intricate possibilities of movement and changing viewpoint. All this can be sympathetically foreseen by the architect, and provided for with infinite diversity. The journey of the eye which does not involve movement of the body provides perhaps the most important aesthetic experiences in architecture. A zone may be occupied, used in fact, if it is visually available. One does not have continually to walk the length of a terrace or mount a flight of steps to justify their laying. The eye is more alert than the body, and much in architecture provides for its activity.

Most architecture is not tailored to the individual but designed for more general use. Even housing is usually 'off-the-peg', or consists of repeated units of various kinds grouped in blocks or layouts which may be intended for differing income groups rather than differing individuals. The individually designed house is probably a relic of aristocratic privilege, and as such may tend to become more of an anachronism as time goes on and communities increase in size. Standardization must inevitably play a large part in accommodation as it does in every other of our needs and amenities, but should be seen rather as an

2. The Campo dei Miracoli at Pisa: the cemetery lies to the left of the other buildings (see page 108)

easy availability of high-level design than as a rigid conformity to arbitrary patterns.

Does architecture emerge as an art? There is no use requiring from it an experience similar to that which a painting, for instance, may offer. We do not require from architecture that demonstration of spiritual and emotional conflict that may be the proper character of other arts. Architectural resolution must be different because the whole *raison d'être* is different, the way we experience it is different, our bodily relation to it is infinitely different. But we must not fall into the common trap of seeing it as a compromise engendered by its threefold obligation. The provision of adequate accommodation can only be afforded through adequate constructive means. It is these processes which themselves satisfy our emotional as well as our material needs. One cannot conceive of architecture without meaningful space and mass. But only when it becomes a unity of habitation is it a full experience.

The Architect as Artist

For some people the difficulty of seeing architecture as art might well be the difficulty of seeing an architect as an artist. This has something to do with temperament. Temperament does not necessarily rage through the arts like a forest fire. The traditional temperament of the prima donna relates to the use of the physical body as the instrument in the performing arts. One does not visualize a novelist or a composer working in a continuous fervour. But even the Greeks saw the poet as torn by the gods, and we must expect responsive nerves if we expect sensitive fingertips. Probably the great architect carries as much temperament as any artist. If we consider the front ranks of twentieth-century architects, Le Corbusier and Frank Lloyd Wright, to name two, we should have no difficulty in fitting them in with this concept of the artist. It is the lesser men that seem to let down that concept. The average architectural firm of today with its teeming offices and brisk personnel presents a scene characteristically different from a group of painters or sculptors, however indifferent the quality of their work, meeting on a project or in a studio. Since this is the rank and file of the profession, it is that part of it with which people most often come in contact.

The architect today is first, it seems, a professional man. He cannot, and this is of fundamental importance, see his project through on his own. Its physical making is in the hands of a vast number of contributory trades, crafts, and even professions. He has, however, to see it through, and this has necessitated (as in fact the process of designing itself necessitates) his familiarity with, and understanding of, every trade involved. More than that, he should be aware of the limits of potential in all these trades so that he himself can exploit and even extend them in creative designing. Architects have understood this desideratum and its implications from their first emergence as the controlling agent in the construction of buildings. Vitruvius, probably no more than an indifferent architect himself, if we judge by the fact that his name is not connected with any distinguished buildings that we know of,* and certainly not outstanding as a writer, lists the qualifications and abilities he thinks necessary to the architect. 'Let him', he says,

> be educated, skilful with the pencil, instructed in geometry, know much history, have followed the philosophers with attention, understand music, have some knowledge of medicine, know the opinions of the jurists, and be acquainted with astronomy and the theory of the heavens.[4]

He goes on to explain the importance to architects of these branches of study. Taking into consideration the limits of knowledge in all spheres at the time, this learning was probably by no means impossible of attainment to the educated man. Vitruvius explains that the architect does not need to be a specialist in each field, but only in his own. We are left with the feeling that architecture is not in any sense a calling, but that it is mastered by assiduous training, aided by what he calls (though he does not define it) 'natural ability'.

For all the contemporary architect's readiness to fling Vitruvius to the historians, as a meaty but indestructible bone, he should perhaps remember that he is the only architect to speak to us from the ancient world, that he may have been more individual in his concepts than we tend to suppose, that it was fifteen hundred years before architects spoke again about the principles of architecture and that when they did get around to it they could think of not much more than to repeat Vitruvius, and that finally, after about four hundred more years during which time versions of his work appeared in different languages, he still lives on as the basis for the training of architects in the vast majority of traditional schools. Academic training is under fire from all directions today, and it is perhaps especially important for architects to find out what they are themselves and what they need.

Vitruvius, as we have said, found three requirements for architecture, called by his most recent translator 'durability, convenience, and beauty'.[5] No one through the ages has thought of contradicting this. The first two qualities we have a right to expect from any architect. The third is the most elusive, and involves more subjectivity in its analysis. Styles and fashions can be acquired

---

* But we do not in fact know the architects of any important Roman buildings.

and play a great part in the satisfaction of both architect and client. It has been assumed that the young architect needs instruction for all three of these branches of responsibility, which have been seen as partly separable, but always interdependent. Though it may be argued that it is the aesthetic category that has determined the ultimate value of a building for preservation, it cannot come into consideration without the satisfactory co-existence of the other two. A building must stand, and function, before it can be thought to please.

By the nature of these priorities it comes about that most buildings are built (and presumably have always been built) with utility and cost in mind. The structural considerations are minimal, and the aesthetic is at best pedestrian. Architects who build like this cannot be regarded as artists, and indeed might be horrified to be so considered. Rule of thumb planning and current building practice will get a structure up, and so many structures are required from a purely accommodational point of view that this approach is adequate for most of them.

Now there is no parallel for this in painting and sculpture, where, whatever the requirements, the *purpose* of the job is visual. Architects seem never to have been unaware of their mixed rôle, and in fact if they have tended to stress any element in their status it has been their concern to be regarded as professional people. Following on after Vitruvius, architects have emphasized the cultural and knowledgeable rather than the artistic background. Alberti considered that the architect 'ought to be a Man of a fine Genius, of a great Application, of the best Education, of thorough Experience, and especially of strong Sense and sound Judgement',[6] though he seemed to repudiate Vitruvius's actual list of required abilities, saying that the 'Arts which are useful, and indeed absolutely necessary to the Architect, are Painting and Mathematicks.' Sir William Chambers in the eighteenth century defined himself as a 'man of business'.[7] From the early nineteenth century institutes have been founded and courses of training and education laid down by which an architect may be recognized as properly qualified. In law he is seen, not as a creative designer, but as the 'agent' appointed to see fair play, as it were, between the builder and the man who is paying for the building. As such he is paid a fee, of which his payment for the *design* of the building forms less than a third. If the contract is cancelled, he is very often not paid at all for the design, even when drawings have been made in some detail, as the client considers he has got nothing so far to pay for. Architects are entitled to submit accounts, even for advice, as lawyers or doctors do, but very often they do not do this because they feel that they would almost always be involved in litigation as a result. Very often in building the architect himself is regarded as redundant, the builder and the quantity surveyor between them are considered quite able to get the building up and work out the accounts for it. Much building is the result of traditional layout and construction methods, and as such can be put up without a skilled designer, and certainly without an *artist* messing around and disturbing everyone's routine. The type of architect produced by the Beaux Arts training in fastidious discrimination of proportions and detailing was a real pain-in-the-neck to the old type of traditional builder, who regarded elaborate instructions about roof-sweeps, chimney mouldings, and window and panelling details, let alone a 'personalized' arrangement of vertical jointing in ashlar masonry, as so much fancy nonsense.

It may well be that some of us can more easily see the architect as an artist in those periods of ornamentation when he was required and expected to produce designs for elaborate ceiling and wall ornaments, fireplaces, wrought ironwork, and even statuary. He very often designed furniture too, to go into his grand houses, and regarded his pieces as at least equal in quality to those of current furniture makers.

In fact the inquiry into the artistic nature of the architect brings us at this point to the not dissimilar question of the artistic standing of other designers; of furniture, for example, of carpets and fabrics, of glass and china, and in our own day, of the status of industrial designers *vis-à-vis* the arts. The only 'minor' art that has often been treated as 'major' is that of ceramic. Hand-made ceramic of course. Many sculptors have used ceramic, either chiefly, or occasionally, as a medium. No recitation is really necessary. The great Della Robbia dynasty in Florence formed one of the most distinguished groups, but there have been others at other times, before and since. Some of the works produced have been the Snake Goddesses of Crete, the life-size figures of the Etruscans, French seventeenth- and eighteenth-century sculptures, works of modern artists like Manzù. These are all easy to accept since they involve only an extension to the common range of sculptors' materials. When we get to pottery vessels it becomes more difficult. In primitive and even bronze age times, vases are our main source of information about the visual arts generally. The painted vases of the Aegean have been accepted as 'high art' of their time. So have the painted vases of Greece, on which we find the signatures of the most illustrious painters of the sixth and fifth centuries—in fact these are almost the only extant works by Greek painters. But the potter too gets a place in the sun. It is generally conceded that the vases must be seriously considered among the art-works of the Greeks. Although the pot is a utilitarian object these painted vases were not household pottery but were made for commemorative or festive celebrations, thus serving a special visual intention in spite of the utilitarian guise. So today —eminent potters do not expect their wares to be used for food storage or preparation, but quite evidently devise and make them in the same spirit in which sculptors work in clay. The prices they fetch suggest their classification. A plate of Picasso's has a meaning quite apart from the functional.

Although fine china and glassware have been collected and admired throughout the ages they have never ranked as 'major' arts, and although today there are distinguished industrial designers the field is classified as 'design' rather than 'art' and not thought of as quite the same thing. Nor of course is furniture, nowadays aligned with industrial design, but an old branch of craftsmanship invading, as has been indicated above, the architect's range of activities. However outworn we may consider the 'Art for Art's sake' concept, we cannot evade the fact that some things are made for use and some purely for visual contemplation and that these things must therefore form different categories. The fact that utilitarian objects may be extremely beautiful and works of art may not be beautiful in this sense at all is of the utmost significance in any attempt to define the meaning of 'art'. There are many activities involving creative imagination which evade classification.

It is generally agreed that a work of art is not merely an orderly arrangement or an imitative likeness, but that in its representations and its arrangements there lies the possibility of evoking emotion, sometimes, in great art, very profound indeed. Vitruvius considered the essential qualities of architecture to lie in order, arrangement, eurythmy, symmetry, propriety, and economy.[8] Can one marshal all these at a high level and yet not have a work of art? Probably one can. So much technical ingenuity is required to make a building that perhaps one's approval is more related to the understanding than the senses. If a sculpture, however pedestrian, is not to be thought of as an 'artwork' it is difficult to decide what it should be regarded as, but people seldom regard buildings, even quite splendid buildings, as works of art.*

Inigo Jones was one of the most distinguished of English architects, and also, for he was a designer of stage settings and a more fluent draughtsman than was customary in his day, may be, of all English architects, the one to whom people might accord the title of 'artist'. His Queen's House at Greenwich says in English what had before been said only in Italian. This is enough to make it historically significant. But what artistic qualities does it have in its own right? Inigo learnt from Palladio. But that generation of northern Italians did not 'invent' the vocabulary they used. It had established itself a hundred years before. The mere use of a style, however chic, is not in itself artistry, though an elegance in handling is an attraction which may promote the building to aesthetic importance. But a work of art, while using the style of its own day, has a character, one can't say independent of the style, but certainly going beyond it.

19

* Especially buildings of their own time and in spite of what has been said above about the Parthenon.

Palladio's distinction was not that he used a vocabulary fashionable in the sixteenth century, but that with that vocabulary, and with planning and structural resources available he achieved a spatial experience (as in his two Venetian churches) or promoted plan arrangements (as in his villas) that resulted in several buildings of distinction and character. Any analysis of Il Redentore is bound to be an aesthetic analysis. The experience of passing through the Mannerist façade and into the nave is one evoking strong sensations.

In domestic work of the sixteenth and seventeenth centuries there was not often, except for very grand houses, the same opportunity to flaunt a dexterity in the handling of contiguous spaces. Palladio's own designs were based primarily on mathematical relations, which may be thought to give a certain dryness to the appearance. This seems to have commended itself to Inigo Jones, for we find a use of the cube for the hall of the Queen's House, a double cube for the Banqueting House, and much later, in the renovations at Wilton, both the cube and the double cube again. The cube itself is invoked purely as an intellectual exercise, for unless the room is very small it will have a height far in excess of that physically necessary. Inigo at Greenwich has used it for the double volume of the hall, where it works beautifully without his having to emulate Italian formal ceiling heights. All Inigo's work is lower than its Italian prototypes, and this becomes a characteristic of English design.

The Queen's House for reasons now never fully explained had to be built 19 across the London–Dover road, thus forming a bridge from the garden to the park. It presented two main façades, one to the park and one to the garden, belonging to the two rectangular blocks on either side of the road (which seems to have required no more than 30 feet of space between the two), and a bridge linked the two blocks at first floor level. The two elevations facing each other were not considered except for a continuation of the regular fenestration throughout the house, and it seems to have been no great architectural loss when the roadway was closed and the house became virtually a large square with two courts.

It may be suggested that the plan of the Queen's House shows all the more attractive qualities of the formal house. The simple symmetry of the rectangle defines the building, which has only two floors. It is surrounded by the system of windows referred to above, placed with reference to each other and the elevation as a whole, and finished with a flat balustraded roof: great chimneys, not hidden away, but as classical as symmetry can make them, begin a new kind of English roof. The oval marble stair is supremely graceful. It is supported by substantial masonry in a most un-Italian manner which allows the actual marble spiral to express itself in an unencumbered apparently cantilevered arrangement. (The 'foothold' which the stair has in its solid wall is evident on the plan.) The hall rises through the total height of the house, allowing Inigo to use his Palladio-inspired 'cube'. A loggia appears as a feature in the south front.

Given the window type as a well-designed and efficient light-unit (perhaps never fully adequate in England) the symmetrical layout of plan and elevation works admirably. The architect uses from the beginning a careful system of scale relations, so that his windows, following their predetermined orbit, will mark out appropriate units, two where the room is long, one where it is short or smaller. No windows 'fall' in awkward places, nor do flues descend where they are not wanted. This is, after all, a professional matter, and amateurish mistakes are neither looked for nor found here.

This house started a fashion which survived the development of many an extravaganza in the following generations to become a great style of architecture, as its ancestor born in Renaissance Italy had been. If Inigo, as is still thought in some circles, had anything to do with the design of Lindsay House in Lincoln's Inn Fields,[9] then he had launched something even more original and important, one of the most important types of urban residence ever to be devised. Lindsay House itself does not present a particularly distinguished façade to the square. The house next door, which has been attributed to Leoni, nearly a century later (1730) appears far more elegant. The setting out of windows in the wall space is tauter, the whole thing is more 'collected'. And no wonder. The fact that we can compare houses of such different dates is the most significant thing about it.

The London house, usually called the Georgian house, has been described and analysed by John Summerson.[10] He points out how ingeniously long and narrow (and therefore economical) sites are planned both to conform, and thus provide continuous and consistent street and square frontages, and to be sufficiently flexible to serve, as a type, both the well-to-do and the very modest income group. In some areas the sites are broader and deeper, and the houses four-storeyed; in others the street-front is smaller, and there may be no more than two storeys. This has become 'anonymous' architecture. If we know the names of any of its architects, it is usually because they have distinguished themselves elsewhere, or have produced a particularly notable interior design, like Robert Adam's ingeniously devised sequences.*

p143

If the Georgian house tended towards anonymity, however, this could not have been said of the great Elizabethan houses. Summerson has called them, happily, 'prodigies'[11] and this surely is what they are, for similarity in building technique and stylistic tendencies of the age have not prevented the production of a number of masterpieces, of which we may take Hardwick Hall in Derbyshire as an example. There is little about this house that could be called

18

* e.g. at 20 St. James's Square.

anonymous, though its whole format is essentially Elizabethan. We are not even sure who designed it, but it seems to have been Robert Smythson.[12] We know that the authoritative and dominating Elizabeth, Countess of Shrewsbury, ordered its erection, and no doubt laid down what was to be done. But a layman, however dictatorial, cannot make an architectural design, and whoever devised the arrangement and proportions of Hardwick was a professional.

It is not a pretty house.[13] It is far too uncompromising for that. It is basically rectangular with six similar rectangular bays, two projecting from each long front, and one from each end. The windows proclaim the relative importance of what lies behind them. There is a squat basement at ground level with a covered 'loggia' on both sides. Above that is a living floor. Above that again is the main reception floor with high windows. These windows are the characteristic plain transomed and mullioned windows of the time, stretching as widely between supporting piers as possible. There is barely a concession here to what may have been learnt of classical wall-area and its orderly progression from basement to attic. Not that the arrangement is disorderly in any respect. In fact there is more than a hint of 'Mannerist' forcing in the symmetry of the two ends of the block.[14] On the other hand the rising of the six bays for an extra floor above the roof level of the central block is in an English tradition. The great hall has receded to play a secondary rôle, or rather no rôle at all, in determining the character of plan or elevation, but is simply contained in the rectangular block.

But by some perceptive prescience the great rooms on the main floor have proportions that outwit classical equivalents. It has been said of the gallery that it is the 'finest room in England',[15] and although such a claim is too subjective to be substantiated it is not made without some justification. A stone stair of unusual felicity links the lower with the second floor.

Perhaps it is a certain informality arising from the origins of the plan in asymmetric zoning that enables these houses to develop original character in spite of a final symmetry and the applied control of façades influenced by Italy. In Italy itself even the most bucolic settings do not counteract the stamp of Renaissance grandeur which is their salient character. One is more likely to meet there than in England that lofty arch or frowning pediment making an impact of monumental masonry which is the counterpart of the sensory attack of sculpture, painting and music. For one must not underestimate this effect of the material of building. Even the small villas of Palladio are set out with a punctilious formality which is never quite emulated in England, where the 'villa' in the Italian sense does not become a characteristic genre. Great country houses of the seventeenth and eighteenth centuries exploit a derivative formal grandeur perhaps proper to their size, and there are of course direct imitations of Palladio's villas which import the Italian manner. A house which particularly

fascinated English architects was the Villa Capra outside Vicenza, most intellectually devised and therefore perhaps most Mannerist of them all. It surmounts
a hill, which provided an excuse for its square plan about the cylindrical domed
hall, with identical faces, each with its pedimented portico looking over the
surrounding country. The high basement enables these to be designed each
with a monumental flight of steps, so that the portico becomes a Roman temple
front. Of course this is not a residence in the full sense, but a *villa suburbana*,
meant for day excursions and popular in the sixteenth century.*

It was later emulated in England by Chiswick House, built by Lord Burling-
ton to serve a similar function, but in Mereworth Castle in Kent, Colen Campbell
repeated Palladio's Rotonda even more closely, introducing bedrooms and
dressing-rooms, however, on the two flanks, which made entrances on these sides
impracticable. The steps are omitted and the porticos become distressingly
overstated loggias. As a small conceit the copy of Palladio is admissible in Mannerist
terms: forced to perform the function of a dwelling it becomes something less than a
work of art. The smoke circulating through the flues concealed in the dome and
emitted by the lantern-chimney is the final ludicrous touch.

In eighteenth-century philosophy, when the beautiful was still explained
largely in classical terms, and referred only to the complete and definitive,
overweening nature—storms, waterfalls, cliffs, ravines, the ocean, rocks, and
mountain ranges were categorized as manifestations of the sublime. Getting
ready for the Romantic Movement this group could include experiences of the
pleasurably horrid or frightening, thus opening up realms for the extension of
the aesthetic undreamt of by the gentle definitions of the Greeks. This applies,
however, only to the plastic arts. Aristotle's analysis of tragedy as the catharsis
of strong and even alienating emotions surely prepared the way for their
invasion into the visual world. With an important difference: however overwhelming a stage tragedy might be it is controlled by the stage, and by the
limiting factor of the poet's sensibility. Real tragedy was never admitted to
the aesthetic range; real rocks have been. It was assumed by the Greeks that the
beauty of man himself was the same sort of thing as beauty in the visual arts,
which were considered to imitate natural beauty. Of course they did nothing of
the sort. They selected, organized, and re-stated, imposing the intellectual idea
everywhere.

Scholars at one period[16] recognized two levels of response in the process of
apprehending beauty: sensation and perception. The sensory response was the
physical one—the assault of sound upon the eardrum or of colour on the eye—
while the percept was in the mind, though reached by information received

* Cf. the Palazzo del Te at Mantua by Giulio Romano.

through the sense organ. It was through perception therefore that shape relations were recognized, and these determined the quotient, as it were, of beauty.
In England Clive Bell and others came forward to say that this (in artworks)
was not merely approval, but the apprehension of an intention, a 'significance',
in the final analysis *moving*.*

One of the difficulties scholars faced was that of isolating emotions arising in
response to beauty (artistic or natural) from those experienced in other situations, particularly in dramatic or tragic situations. It is easy to approve the
relentless Erinyes pursuing a character in a Greek play, though we may weep
when the moment of his destruction is upon us, and because we know it is a
poetic statement, to recognize the difference between our state of mind then
and that in which we may see, or even hear of, the actual killing of a child. But
some plays do shock us, and some moments of reality may give rise to recog-
nizably 'aesthetic' reactions. Of course we do not believe, as Clive Bell's generation did, in a specific 'aesthetic' emotion. We understand merely (as far as we
can) that some emotion rises in response to an aesthetic evocation. We are
hesitant too to speak of beauty. Somehow the aesthetic is more complex than
this. We must stick to the term 'aesthetic' otherwise we shall have no nomen-
clature to link us with the past!

While it is almost impossible to separate, even intellectually, so-called 'sensations' and 'perceptions' in the aesthetic experience of architecture, there does
seem to be a difference in our range of apprehension of the various qualities of a
building, though this may prove to be a difference in degree rather than kind.
For instance the recognition of mathematically or proportionately related
features in the façade of a classical building may win our approval, and even
move us to that 'delight' that Vitruvius and his followers demanded of architecture. But when we come up to a building and are overwhelmed by, say, the
immensity of a rising column of marble, so that the heart beats faster and
engenders ecstatic 'feelings' about the might of human imagination, etc., etc., is
this a totally different experience? It is not simply a stronger one, since size in
itself is not usually regarded as an aesthetic factor.

But it surely should be so regarded, especially when deliberately invoked by
the human mind and hand. The term sublime was used for manifestations that
defied analysis and assessment: therefore the very large, or the very wild, or the
very disorderly (in human terms). Attempts to imitate them in art, whether in
painting or construction, have usually led to the ludicrous. But there is no
doubt that a sublime quality in its own right has often been achieved in a work
of art. In Baroque art, for example. Or by the Egyptians. Or perhaps by   p13
painters like Picasso. A sheer wall of undeterminable width and height, rising   5, 6, 7, 8, 56

* The concept of 'Significant Form', so long central to English art criticism.

before one, causes a strong emotional reaction, like that caused by a rock-face. So does a wall of glass, apparently not there at all. This is a different emotion, less violent but not necessarily less profound. There is almost no aspect of architectural design that cannot be used to provoke a strong emotion. That we walk past and through so many buildings without feeling any is a comment on the remarkable efficiency of most people at producing the nondescript. 'A lovely home', people say, not 'a lovely *house*', which they do not mean. Only architects do not say it. They tend to say nothing, and seldom praise one another's designs, perhaps because there is rarely anything to praise. The architect may say 'What a marvellous site', thereby suggesting his own and everybody else's awareness of futility.

Anonymous Architecture

All valid building reflects the design and constructional manner of its own day: to this extent it is 'anonymous'. Anonymity does not merely mean that we have lost the name of the architect, or that it was never known, or that there was no architect: it means that it has so few distinguishing marks of the individual designing hand that these are unimportant in its stylistic classification. It means that it is not, in itself, uniquely distinguished or seminal. In this sense the 10 greater part of all building is anonymous. Greek temples are virtually anony- 29 mous though we may have the names of their architects. The Pantheon in Rome is not anonymous though we do not know who designed it. The Greek temple has a plan and proportions characteristic of its time and place. The Pantheon is a unique demonstration of individual brilliance. This is not to prefer the Pantheon to the Parthenon in a value-assessment, but merely to state a classifi- p30 catory difference. First of all, in the Pantheon, comes the concept of the vast p131 dome upon its cylinder, creating a new spatial statement in materials developed to make this possible. Internally there is no break or change of direction; the space held in this simple structure is almost palpable. It is defined by the light admitted at the only place structurally inevitable, the thin top of the dome, the thickness necessarily increasing downwards to contain the thrust and transmit it to the walls. The thickness of these is finally asserted and demonstrated by the niches and recesses at its base, which are not so over-emphasized as to weaken its sturdiness, retaining as it does sufficient mass to buttress the enormous weight. Below, the floor paving marks out the area in the directionless continu- ity of the circle. Above, echoing it lightly, floats the disc of light confined in its shining metal band. This imaginative spatial concept had not happened on such a scale before, and was never exactly repeated. Its greatness lies precisely in this spatial design: the structure waits upon it.* This shows the architect as artist.

It is not meant to suggest here that the presence of the architect in individual examples of buildings in any of the great styles, whether Greek or Gothic, is unimportant or undetectable. One has only to analyse the differences among, say, the cathedrals of the thirteenth century to realize the important part played 40 by individual decision. But one will find the similarities (and I do not speak, though I might, of direct influence) more fundamental than the differences. The architect cannot evade his times. He may look over his shoulder (like the architect of Bourges to Paris) or steadfastly at the job in hand, which is to say forward (like the architect of Chartres) but he does not create meaningful building in a style other than that of his own day.

Here we may consider the 'revival' of styles, and first the first of them, the controversial Renaissance. From the fifteenth century onwards architects were avowedly turning to ancient Rome for their forms. Vitruvius, who had produced the only known Roman text of architectural precept, was the model, not only for theorists of the fifteenth and sixteenth century in Italy, but, chiefly through them, for those of the seventeenth and eighteenth centuries too throughout the western world.

Vitruvius was evidently conservative for he refers to Greek and Roman methods as one continuous manner, the Roman merely providing the later practice. As he wrote before the beginning of the Christian era, we have nothing from him of domes or barrel or cross vaults (structural developments that for us characterize Roman architecture as against Greek) nor of course reference to buildings like the great baths, palaces, and vaulted basilicas. Neither the Pantheon nor the 29, 52 Colosseum was built in his lifetime, though he was clearly aware of some of the colonial enterprises, perhaps including the marvellous buildings of the Augustan age in the south of France. It is just possible that he saw the arch as a 11 construction rather utilitarian than formal. It is strange that he hardly discusses the arch or vault with voussoirs at all. He seems to have been a generation older than Augustus, though, and might not have lived to see the most important of these. Certainly architects of the fifteenth century could have got nothing from him of the vault or dome, the great determinants of Renaissance style.

The cross-vault in its ribbed form, both semi-circular and pointed, was known from medieval buildings in Northern Italy. The Gothic arch had not made such an inroad in the thirteenth and fourteenth centuries that one could regard the use of the semi-circular arch and vault as a revival proper, since it was probably continuous. But Brunelleschi and Alberti both went to Rome, and there they saw p30, p131 not only the Pantheon, with its breathtaking demonstration of what could be done

* See also pp. 44 and 75.

with a dome, but the Roman arches and barrel vaults, mathematically organized and adjusted with advanced technical skill, and also the Roman cross vault, unobscured by ribs, and built on a scale never equalled by the medieval world.

No wonder that world seemed clumsy and retrograde. Everywhere too was the elegant reminder of classical formality: the unit of arch flanked by attached columns, supporting their superimposed series of entablatures, and creating a subtle visual framework imposed upon the structural veracity of arch and vault. 52

Brunelleschi filled Florence with buildings that demonstrated his understanding of the Roman achievement, and crowned the cathedral with a great 32 dome, from the summit of which his other works may be clearly made out. Superficially this dome may not appear to resemble that of the Pantheon. He had not the technical resource of concrete,* nor the practical advantage of a continuous wall upon which to rest his dome. But he seems to have understood the underlying 'rib' principle of the Roman construction, and this is the principle of his own dome.† (The double skin of the dome may have been suggested by the double dome of the octagonal baptistry opposite.)

Alberti was the analytical theorist. He had written a treatise on painting (1436) and later (1452) one on architecture, in which he takes his departure from Vitruvius, with his own development of the Roman theory. But before this was published in 1485 (after his death) he had designed his formal façades for Florence and Rimini, and built his two churches in Mantua.

We may reflect at Sant'Andrea in Mantua how Roman, how very Roman, 12 was his thinking. But the Romans did not use the barrel vault over the main p135 zone of a building, possibly because, even with concrete, the cross vault developed less thrust. Alberti, having only masonry—in this case brick—had to buttress his great vaulted nave, which he did very adequately by the use of side chapels,‡ forming his unit of arch and pier in the nave elevation, repeated in the porch. The extra height caused by the barrel vault carries the circular window which appears so oddly above and behind the west front, but seems to have been intended to be set into a gabled wall. It is sometimes forgotten that this is the first barrel-vaulted nave in Italy: certainly the first to be handled with such formality. One wonders where he got it, and whether he could have known of the barrel vaults of Romanesque France.§ He must have felt strongly that a cross-vaulted nave was

---

* The Roman understanding of this useful material had been lost, although the Renaissance builders in Italy did use rubble and mortar inside the wall-faces.

† See also p. 45.

‡ A buttressing system not dissimilar in fact to that used in the Basilica of Constantine.

§ There are in fact Romanesque barrel vaults in Italy, e.g. in Prato Cathedral, here interrupted by the windows of the clerestory, as they were also used in France, giving the effect of a continuous cross-vaulted nave. Alberti himself had used a barrel vault in the Chapel of the Holy Sepulchre in S. Pancrazio in Florence.

3. The Pantheon, Rome (see pages 75–6)

the wrong approach to a domed crossing, for although he had designed the less important San Sebastiano as a centralized church with very short arms, he does not give the impression of recognized defeat at Sant'Andrea. Rather there is a confidence, an assurance, in the carefully calculated relations there.

All Renaissance architects were clearly very conscious of the west front of a basilican church as a problem. Their concern to give a Roman stamp to the main façades of their buildings is probably responsible for their reputation as imitators and their unpopularity among critics who feel that the advance of architectural design was halted by this determined nostalgia for antiquity. They recognized Roman formality in temple portico and triumphal arch. The basilica, just as much a Roman form as the others, a practical method of creating a large well-lit place of assembly, and used for churches right through the Middle Ages (therefore not in itself a turning back), presented a formal problem because the designers of the fifteenth and sixteenth centuries wanted to invest it with a character it had not originally possessed. The end of a secular basilica had not been particularly significant externally as it became when the type of building was adopted by the early Christian church and developed to serve ritual rather than practical purposes.

What the Renaissance was doing was to use the pattern of Roman elevational treatment (the decorative combination of arches framed in applied orders) instead of continuing the Gothic development of pointed arch and stone tracery. In so doing they set aside the elaboration of flying buttresses and external piers (which had never, it must be remembered, been used in Italy) for the taste of humanist rationality. The barrel vault could, in the event, span a wider nave than was achieved by Gothic bays,* and the vault that had sym-bolized medieval aspiration was no longer as appropriate as the dome, the vault of heaven, which was recognized again as reflecting itself in terrestrial things as God was manifest in Man. The mathematics of the cosmos was eagerly simulated in music and architecture as was supposed to have been done before the invasion of barbarism. One should not allow the use of the Roman orders to mislead one too easily into recognizing a retrogression in architectural thinking. Even when a façade (like that of San Carlino in Rome †) almost exactly recalls another designed in antiquity, this does not imply a repetition, as materials and manner of construc-tion may differ, and the façade treatment may simply be a stylistic superficiality. Certainly the plans do not follow a Roman prototype, though they may, as in the case of the basilica, continue a type first established by the Romans.

marginal note: 11, 22, 29 / 7, 8

---

* Sant'Andrea in Mantua 60 ft., Amiens *c.* 50 ft.
† San Carlo alle Quattro Fontane, Rome, by Borromini. Its façade is very much like a rock-cut temple at Petra. See also p. 56.

This applies very clearly to house and villa. Nobody would wish to maintain that the emergence of the Renaissance town house, with or without a central cortile, is in any way a step retrograde to the design of the medieval house in Italy. The villa disappears in a feudal society, and is revived only with the return, if one can call it that, of an educated bourgeoisie or at least upper middle class as opposed to nobility. The villas of Palladio, though his clients may have been stimulated into requiring them partly by writers like Virgil talking of his own, had no extant Roman examples to follow, and had to be conceived and designed in their entirety by the architect.

The transfer of the Palladian villa to England indicates a different degree of derivation and emulation. In the hands of Inigo Jones it is a conscious attempt to advance according to the lead of an accepted older master. Palladio and his contemporaries as a group determined the direction that would be taken by English domestic architecture a century and a half later.* Some of these English Palladians were distinguished architects, but hardly perhaps great artists; men certainly of sensibility, but not of the calibre, any of them, of a Brunelleschi; not that we are concerned with comparing talents, but with indicating that an architect may be accomplished without producing a great building. The anonymity of the works, if not of the men, is hard to break through. Once someone has made something it is reasonably easy for someone else to make a similar thing as good, or even better.

The eighteenth century everywhere, especially in its town house, but in all its buildings, which retain an essential simplicity in planning, shows a reaffirmation after the excesses of the Baroque and Rococo, of the orderly arrangements of Renaissance classical vocabulary; this rather than revival, less of a revival even than that of the quattrocento. Especially perhaps in England Georgian urbanity takes its place beside the great 'anonymous' styles of the past. We may recognize the signature of a James Gibbs here or Robert Adam there, just as the specialist may demonstrate a difference in manner between Ictinus and Callicrates (the architects of the Parthenon), but for most people the Georgian house is almost a vernacular, perhaps being first devised by Inigo Jones and his followers, and then developed and standardized as the type of English town house. The Gothic revival, and all the 'revivals' of the late eighteenth and nineteenth centuries, Greek, Egyptian, Indian, Chinese, were either a mere scratching at the surface of established practice to produce a voguish effect, or the production of pieces which, though more individual, led neither to great architecture nor even distinguished anonymity. The Brighton Pavilion was first designed as a Regency-Classical building, and when the 'oriental' style was

* Inigo Jones: 1573–1652; Palladio: 1508–80; Palladians active 1710–50.

adopted no alterations to the plan were necessary, while examples like Fonthill Abbey or Strawberry Hill are curiosities rather than masterpieces.

An architect is necessary to most building chiefly in his technological rôle: producing working drawings (even specifications are occasionally drawn up by quantity surveyors), organizing services such as plumbing, lighting, heating, making what individual changes and deviations are necessary to pedestrian and derivative plan layouts, devising minimally adequate elevations, choosing among an ever-increasing variety of available accessories (windows, door furniture, light fittings, extractor fans). Some big building concerns keep their own design consultant (he may not be called an architect, whose name is protected by law deriving from a professional charter*) to supply all these requirements. The architect has today a long and packed training in which design, his major subject, means not creative art but experience in organizing, zoning, grouping, arranging, much of which can be learnt. Obviously a man of sensibility will be a better architect, a man of talent a good architect; a man of genius who can bend to his creative intentions the many materials and trades that impede the lesser man alone will produce great architecture.

Simple standard building practice, which produces adequately functioning buildings (especially houses, but nowadays even big commercial and industrial buildings), without benefit of a qualified architect (though a draughtsman is always necessary) can result in a composite effect not unlike vernacular. It is in fact very difficult to define the 'upper' limits of vernacular, if we see its fundamental quality in the simplicity of standardized living units (for example the igloo or the African tribal hut and kraal), each unit or group of units actually constructed by the individuals or families who will use them. If we extend this simple classification to include, for example, Mediterranean houses (the clusters of cottages on Greek islands, the Trulli in southern Italy), or Pueblo villages in Mexico (where each unit makes use of its existing neighbour as partial support and protection), without advanced technology, we are moving towards specialization, where people are builders by trade, and towards an increased complexity of unit which produces the stone hamlets of Provence, the Italian hill towns (perhaps with some formal building around the main piazza) and alpine villages in many areas of Switzerland and its immediate neighbours. The group would have included almost all Elizabethan towns and villages, where no 'individual' architects were employed, and where the variety in buildings (again mostly domestic) represented what we might call standard deviation.

Except for the building of people technologically undeveloped, 'primal'

* An architect who is such by being a member of his Institute may not legally be affiliated with any building trade. There is no law however to prevent his brother-in-law, or even his brother, doing so!

building as it were, we can often recognize in a vernacular type the formal prototype from which it is derived, as a dialect or patois derives from a formal language. It may presumably therefore have originally been architect-devised, but it retains only the general statement, hence its anonymity. It has little meaning as a single unit. Its character is a group character. It is what is called in some art-circles a *multiple*, that is to say there is no longer any original or prototype. Its repeatability is an essential part of its character. It is natural for dwellings to exist in groups or clusters, as it is natural for people to form communities for convenience and protection; therefore one may expect visual conformity in any one group of units. That is why vast apartment houses, though repellent to many, are an inevitable contemporary solution to housing in areas of dense population. In principle not very different from, say, the massing of a pueblo, they afford the opportunity for a standard of efficient organization of essential services, down to the last provision of a community centre, that has become impossible today in any other planning system where space is at a premium.

Anonymity is not of course any key to the quality of buildings. If we agree in regarding the Greek temple, and the Renaissance and Georgian town houses as belonging to this category we shall see that some of the types established and continued for hundreds of years can be very fine indeed. But not all buildings repeated in large numbers are admirable. The semi-detached houses that extend like an infection along so many miles of English roads, for example, have no quality except that of providing shelter for thousands of families. (There is little architectural justification for the semi-detached house; the terrace house is another matter.) Worse than that (for we do not bother to refer to the simply negative in style), they maintain a tradition of ugliness so widespread that people come to regard it as normal. One stage removed from these is that suburban house on a small plot whose owners believe it to be different from its neighbours. Varying in details, perhaps it may be, but not significantly different. And why should it be? The function of a dwelling among similar class or income groups can scarcely have elastic limits on a 50 × 100 foot plot. Sad as it may be for architecture when professional architects have no great imaginative gifts, it is much sadder when the non-professional turns to designing—or even altering—a building. Knocking down walls, closing in porches and verandas, replacing small but appropriate windows with picture windows when there are, alas, no pictures to be framed, turning a modest little box into a pretentious monster; which is worse, this or the subdivision of gaunt old houses into unseemly hardboard flats? The point usually made is that they were never much, or were even ugly, before. Now they may be worse, because they have forgone even what character they were intended to have.

The Architect as Engineer

As early as 1716 a Department of Bridges and Roads was created in France, of which the chief 'engineer' was the architect, Jacques Gabriel. It was thus a branch of architecture and was at first staffed and operated by personnel with architectural training. By the middle of the century the *Ecole des Ponts et Chaussées* had been established for their special instruction, but it was still expected that they would have some architectural experience. The first director, Charles Perronet, was an architect. For some time there was no real indication of the emergence of a separate profession of engineering though there had been a much earlier awareness of the advantage of using mathematical calculation in the working out of structural design. John Smeaton (1724–1792) was probably the first Englishman to refer to himself as a 'Civil Engineer', and a Society of Civil Engineers was in fact established in 1771, though training courses for civil engineers were not offered at British universities until 1840.

The first use of the designation civil engineering had been to distinguish the work, not from what was called civil architecture, but from military engineering, now seen as perhaps the lesser part of the activity of constructing roads, bridges, and large-scale communications generally. Civil architecture was in any case poor stuff during the late eighteenth century, and offered little opportunity to designers, reared as they were in the great classical tradition. If we look back now we shall find that any real challenge in designing, well into the nineteenth century, occurred only in the field of bridges, canals, and large structures in iron and glass for conservatories and like purposes. During the later nineteenth century this emphasis intensified, and the development of steam power, and industry generally, prompted factory and warehouse design, and, important for style, construction, and town layout, the railway station. So that while domestic work continued in a spate of degenerating repetition, advance was made in response to the new industrial challenge.

Even before the middle of the nineteenth century the divergence in direction between architects and engineers was beginning to cause anxiety. Although the architects themselves were among the most concerned, their own muddled attitude towards the proper scope of architectural responsibility, and their inability to envisage a change in aesthetic standpoints to meet the new accommodational and structural developments did nothing to halt the widening of the rift. The architect continued to vacillate between resentment and scorn at the scope of the engineer's preserve, while the latter took the only possible retaliatory attitude of patronage which is so easily provoked by an assumption of exclusiveness on the part of the artist.

From Roman times architects had been as much concerned with military architecture as civil, and civil architecture itself differed from domestic building to the extent that the provision of large covered areas for the use of great crowds of people involved structural enterprise and skill. There were, moreover, buildings of public utility like aqueducts and bridges, which provided essential services in peace-time as well as times of campaigning. The gates in a city wall were as capable of monumental treatment as a triumphal arch and any building made without pressure of exigency was subject to its appropriate share of formality and pomp. It has been said too glibly that the Romans were engineers rather than architects; this statement becomes meaningless if we look at Roman buildings. That kind of thinking suggests that when a building involves constructional complexity instead of merely sensitivity to the proportional and decorative relation of parts, it thereby forfeits its right to be considered as architecture. By the time Rome was being thus critically analysed Greece had become the ideal, and the sufficiency of its crystal simplicity, its crisp colonnades, its philosophy of the temperate, and its unambitious social structure showed up what had become in Roman hands the clutter of excess, the tension of structural audacity, the zest for empire.

Vitruvius almost anticipates nineteenth-century architectural precept when he ignores the great structural advances of his day,* while laboriously analysing the proper disposition of the parts of a Greek order. In Greek building the column formed, with lintel and wall, the whole structural vocabulary. Plans were largely standardized, and architecture was a question of finesse: the shaping and placing of the various parts to form an incomparably inter-related whole. The Roman architect was faced with a far more advanced, if less delicate, problem.

Architecture begins with the requirement of the provision of adequate space or spaces. The decision as to what is adequate is, or should be, largely the architect's. The space considered adequate for the shrine of a goddess could vary according to circumstances or siting from the tiny cube of Nike Apteros to the vast naos of the Parthenon, or the still greater inner chambers of Sicilian temples. The proportions of the members and the system of construction hardly changed. If dimensions were required which a single lintel could not easily span, intermediate supports were introduced, as in the Parthenon and at Paestum in Italy. Quite a different situation arises in designing the great rooms of Roman baths. Here free space is required for the continuous movement of many people. Only a vaulted system can be contemplated, and this affects the whole character of the building.

The use of arch and vault had been established before this. The lack of ready stone and the availability of suitable clay had led naturally to brick rather than

p129

* Though most features that we recognize as especially Roman are of a rather later day than his.

stone construction, and the increase of its flexibility as a structural material was promoted by the development of a mortar and rubble mix that became a good concrete. The brick arch and vault, aided by concrete, led to the establishment of a system of vaulting which not only developed little thrust but was reasonably light.

The old question arises here of whether a structural system develops to serve a practical or aesthetic need, or whether structural developments promote style usage and spatial facility. This is exactly where the great architect comes in. He is a person who devises, in terms of materials and building methods available to him, a spatial excursion which extends and exploits them to their limits. Then those limits will need to be expanded and redefined. This is what happened p131 with the dome of the Pantheon. After that the only possibility of extension p132 became the dome on pendentives, as at Santa Sophia. (These two domes are closer than may at first appear. In the Pantheon the dome actually rests on 'piers' of solid masonry from which linking arches spring to lighten the load over the recesses in the walls. Santa Sophia represents a culmination, as the Pantheon itself did.) Building developments may well have been going on in more pedestrian buildings: the architect, however imaginative, can gather into his control only *existing* facilities, however scattered. They are extended while pressing to interpret his ideas. Material structure is what an architect uses to provide accommodation. There are not two things, the design and the structure, it is the structure that is designed. There is no one there but the designer (or design group) until the project is handed over to the army of workmen who will carry out his instructions. If there are structural advances to be made, he will make them. If structure is to present new kinds of spaces, it will be by his vision and direction that this is done.*

The technical knowledge required for the design of buildings in Roman times could easily be acquired by one man. Even in the late fifteenth century and on through the sixteenth a 'many-sided' scholar, like Alberti or Leonardo, could know what was known. A man like Michelangelo could be responsible for p13 designing one of the greatest domes in western architecture, and, though the most distinguished (and busy) sculptor and painter of his day, yet find time to write sonnets.

During the Middle Ages knowledge, especially structural knowledge, was even more confined. (Many Roman skills had been lost, including the making of concrete.) By the eleventh century the materials used were brick, sometimes plastered, and stone, often finely carved in capital, moulding, or tympanum. Walls were load bearing, thick, and reinforced with buttresses. Roofs were simple timber trusses, or they were vaulted with cross or barrel vaults. Domes

* 'Structure' should not be confused with 'construction'. See also p. 40.

were not very large, and rested on the clumsier squinch rather than pendentives. Churches of this date tend to fall into two classes, the kind I have called
'anonymous' architecture, which would include, for example, the pilgrimage
churches of southern France, and another kind, perhaps of more technical
precision, which show greater sophistication. One of these is St. Front at
Périgueux, an immaculate series of domes on pendentives covering a Greek
cross, built at the same time as St. Mark's at Venice, and obviously not acciden-
tally related to it in plan.

Yet when the structural advance came it was made in the development of the
long-naved basilica, and domed construction was set aside over all Europe,
because the new system was based on the pointed vault. Here the question is
usually, did the architect devise the pointed arch to express spiritual aspiration,
or was he excited by the discovery of its ability to reach greater height by reason
of its lesser stresses?* In the French Gothic cathedrals the actual arch forms a
relatively small part of the total height. The structural achievement was surely
the supporting pier and the development of a masonry technique which bound
the members adequately into the basic pier. Not the least of the calculations
necessary for the final equilibrium must have been the balance of the prop of
the flying buttress against the outward-tending weight of the nave wall, and the
inward buckling that would result from any pressure applied from without. As
time passes stone settles and mortar hardens, until eventually a nearly monolithic fabric finds its own equilibrium. Buttresses have come apart today without
disaster to the rest of the building, but this could hardly have been calculated!

In contrast to the bony insistence of the cathedrals one tends to think of
Renaissance buildings, and Renaissance in the expansive sense, from St. Peter's
to St. Paul's and from Vicenza to Versailles, as buildings without structural
significance, with tidy classical faces and symmetrical disposition. This is true
as far as the continued use of load-bearing walls is concerned, but in their way
the barrel and groin vaults are as much in control as the rib had been of the
spatial character of the building: a less spectacular affair than Gothic aspiration,
but as positive. Of the medieval world we have little more than the churches,
but of the Renaissance world we have also splendid though not structurally
complex secular buildings. Above all we have the return of palace and villa in
the grand manner. The assured manipulation of vault and dome is joined by a
far more elaborate system of planning than has been found since Rome, and one
not surprisingly related to the manner of antiquity, though more complex in its
employment of several storeys in the great houses.

---

* It has been held in question whether the pointed arch does ultimately develop more vertical
compression than the semi-circular. In any event it is what they then believed that is relevant here.

We may say that the main architectural contribution during the sixteenth and seventeenth centuries was in the relating of shapes: the breaking down of the sober classical block into articulated wings and pavilions, the development of the villa and country house, and the inclusion of parks and gardens into the whole architectural scheme. The architect's structural abilities are not often marshalled here. Except, of course, for the dome. The Renaissance in Italy, one might say, was heralded by a dome, the dome of Florence Cathedral. Brunelleschi designed this dome to crown fittingly the crossing of a medieval church. He uses what is basically a rib construction, upon which a double membrane depends, and he pulls up the crown of the dome into that unique pointed curve that is the touch of genius. His problem was not so much a structural as a constructional one. He could not, as architects might today, leave it to an engineer to calculate and a building contractor to put up. The difficulty was that he wanted to raise it on a drum, which brought the springing point up to 180 feet above floor level (higher than the highest point of Beauvais' vault) and the diameter was 138 feet. Not even St. Peter's was to exceed this. The problem was a builder's problem: how to erect scaffolding and centring? It could not be done. So the architect had to design a dome that could be built without them. The double thickness of the dome with the thicknesses linked by supporting ribs made this possible. Workmen once up there had to stay for the whole day, and canteens were provided at drum level to feed them.

A problem more truly of engineering confronted Wren in his designing of the dome of St. Paul's. Following in the tradition of having a dome of two thicknesses, most specifically here to afford as great an external loftiness as feasible, Wren devised a system using a particularly light outer shell of wood, which would not have been substantial enough to support the lantern. This therefore rests on a conical structure, between the two domes and emerging from the main springing. Wren seems almost to have enjoyed practising a certain measure of deception in concealing his structural devices, for the buttresses propping up the nave roof are tucked away behind a bland classical façade. Also neither of his dome peristyles, inner or outer, defines the true position of the base of the dome (which is 112 feet in diameter as against St. Peter's 137 feet 6 inches).

It almost seems to be at the point where architecture is making the least spectacular use of structural skills, that the civil engineer becomes defined as a separate entity. This cannot be entirely accidental. When the 'social' preoccupations of the architect are largely concerned, as they were in the late eighteenth century, with niceties of disposition, with ornament and furniture, with gardens and summerhouses, and with the superficial revival of past styles, it would surely have been little short of alarming to suggest to him that his proper business was to prepare for the new century by turning his attention to canals and bridges, railway stations and warehouses. Some of these had hitherto been a military concern. Now all were to be the concern of the new profession. This shift of emphasis was a source of corruption in the world of architecture from which it has not yet wholly rid itself. Architects found they were increasingly incapable of the mathematical training required for structural design, while engineers regarded the architect as the man who would provide the ornamental part. By and large it is only the backward aesthetic of the engineer that has kept the architect in business at all.[17] He is excluded from anything not requiring ornament. This explains what often (and increasingly) indicates his redundancy today, and is to a large measure his own fault. It took a Le Corbusier, a virtually unique figure in the first half of this century, to reassert the rôle of the architect in devising a building, and to find himself capable of directing its construction.

The Engineer as Architect

In recent years there has been increasing evidence of the engineer's unwillingness to settle for the younger brother's portion and of his claiming for himself a share as large, if not (as with Esau) larger. Not only does he lay claim (through his spokesman, the engineering 'historian') to the best and most important buildings of antiquity, but he implies with equal imperturbability that their designers were his own forbears. He has bagged the whole of Egypt and the Aegean, and while (reluctantly) giving the architect the Parthenon, lays claim to the whole of Rome (except the ornament), Santa Sophia, Chartres, and 28, 40 Amiens. He is indifferent about the Renaissance (except of course for vaults, domes, and bridges) and by the nineteenth century has emerged anyway in his own right with the Crystal Palace and the Eiffel Tower. Since then it has been 41 plain sailing. Though most of us will do little more than blink at the forced surrender of Imhotep,* we do sit up nervously when Vitruvius is referred to as a Roman engineer, and his treatise is described as 'a long book on engineering construction or, as he called it, architecture'.[18] Later the same writer says

> one feels somehow free to consider the Roman structures as engineering, done by men who had something of an engineering training, whereas there is a tendency to feel that the Gothic cathedrals are the product of inspired architecture, in the modern rather than the ancient engineering sense, and inspired building. It is enigmatic that the earliest man-made

---

* Architect in Dynastic Egypt.

structures which can be analysed in any real sense by modern theory, and that only by engineers, may have had little content that can be called engineering.[19]

The term 'engineer', though deriving from the Latin *ingeniatorem*, was not used in the civil engineering sense until the eighteenth century, when it emerged as a special branch of architecture. This curious reluctance now to acknowledge the common background must, one supposes, be due to some form of *amour propre* which is sensitive to a hint of the bar sinister. But why? The common ancestry is more than acceptable to the architect, who indeed is concerned today to save his structural antecedents, and is (we presume) only too anxious to acknowledge, and indeed, on at least some occasions, be identified with his more scientifically trained colleague.

Prior to the emergence of the civil and structural engineer the architect had managed his own structural designing. The engineer presumably emerged when he was needed: that is to say when the development of building materials and structural finesse became too complicated to be fully covered in the architect's training, which remained primarily one of the planning of accommodational relations. A tendency—perhaps more than a tendency—on the architect's part to close his eyes and ears to all but the merest extension of his knowledge in the structural field, clearly served as an encouragement to the development of the specialist in structures, and led to his (the specialist's) and everyone else's identification of the architect as the mere prettifier of structure. For instance Sigfried Giedion refers to Haussmann's inability to find architects to help him in his projects for Paris: 'There were at that date no town planners to aid him in avoiding mistakes' and he found the architects totally inadequate for any sort of practical co-operation.

> They were prepared at best to design single buildings, for erection on sites pointed out by someone else. Architects at this period were like those old-style tragedians who could not have thought they were acting if they had been given prose parts to read.
> Haussmann had to look in other fields for his helpers. And in any case buildings were for him only the *décor de la vie*. From the beginning he looked on his work as a technical problem and carried his real difficulties to the engineers, his closest collaborators.[20]

In this century the architect began to realize where he had landed himself, whether too late or not we are not yet in a position to judge.

Elizabeth Mock[21] has pointed out that the situation is anything but clear-cut since, although the engineer made an unself-conscious contribution in the nineteenth century because it did not occur to him to worry about the aesthetic, as soon as he did start worrying about it his designing became inhibited; whereas the architect, unaware during this early period that he was being left out of anything, is now more aware than the engineer of the aesthetic value of structural forms. Now, finally, the engineer is catching up with an awareness of his own potential which could lead, and indeed has led, to his rejection of the architect in some fields.

What is the difference between architecture and engineering? It has been considered to lie in scale, particularly in the sizes of spans.[22] Do the architect and the engineer merely attend to different aspects of a building, there being buildings which can be structured without one or the other? Has the architect more ingenuity in devising plans and formal space relations, and the engineer more ingenuity in devising systems of cover and support? Is there a fundamental difference between buildings deriving from one approach and buildings deriving from the other? Can an engineer learn the planning techniques and formal aesthetic necessary in contemporary building without sacrificing time he needs for mastering calculation? Can an architect learn to calculate and design structures so that he becomes independent of the engineer? Are both types of training to remain necessary, and shall we continue to play it, as we do now, by ear? That is to say shall we go on leaving the individual decision to the special case? Or will the future belong to those who elect on a permanent partnership basis to collaborate?

Peter Collins, an architect writing in 1965, inclines to the view that

> The distinction between architecture and engineering was not, as Fergusson had claimed, the distinction between a Fine Art and a utilitarian art, but between two types of creative design, whereby the quality of genius required to create beauty was equally meritorious in both instances, and where the distinction of techniques was influenced only by requirements imposed by the need to design for very different spans.[23]

He goes on to say, pertinently, that 'even today we find that any engineer who designs beautiful structures, such as Pier Luigi Nervi, tends to be designated as an architect *honoris causa*'. Perhaps we could go further and suggest that it does not matter whether the designer is an architect or an engineer by profession, so long as the building can be considered a work of architecture, or even art, or whatever classification the future holds for works hitherto grouped under those categories. Modern engineers should not wear a chip on the shoulder about having their work called 'architecture' since, as we have tried to show, the term embraces both a wider and more selective group of structures than would be included in the category 'designed by an architect'. A work of architecture is so by its own quality, whether it has been designed by a professional architect or engineer or both or neither. There are no buildings which do not involve some degree of engineering, nor any engineers' structures which do not involve some building. What kind of specialist the designing of the whole or part of it proceeds from depends on the requirements. It is surely a matter of degree, not kind. Essentially the architect plans and the engineer structures. These activities are not mutually exclusive.

Form has always emerged from structure, but there have been times when the structure, having first suggested suitable forms, has then waited upon them. Such a time was that of classical architecture. It has always been maintained that the Greek orders and their arrangement in a trabeated system constituted a response to the evocative possibilities of marble construction; yet actually none of the Greek temples outside the mainland of Greece, and not all those in Greece itself are made of marble. Where they are not, the smoothness of marble
10 was simulated by the use of a fine stucco, if possible of marble dust, applied over the surface of the building stone, and applied relief sculpture and other details were, if possible, marble. In fact one might justifiably suggest that the finesse of relations common in Greek architecture was not at all appropriate to the sites in, say, Magna Graecia, and that the Roman development of faced concrete was an aesthetic as well as a practical one. When Roman sculptors did work in marble their craftsmanship is often extremely refined, and in their relief carving they characteristically deviated from what the Greeks had brought to such a high level of achievement, by increasing a spatial extension in the representation of depth beyond the surface, which they suggested by making the objects in the distance smaller and in lighter relief. This tendency towards a more ambiguous attitude to space finds obvious expression in mural painting, where panels of wall are often treated as deep space, but also in their usage of applied orders on the elevations of some of their monumental buildings.

Writers tend to dismiss the Roman system of applied orders on the façades of arcuated structures as a superficial 'borrowing' from the Greeks, but if we
52 analyse for example the face of the Colosseum which is of wrought stone over a honeycomb of brick and concrete vaults we shall see that it is in fact a trabeated screen of superimposed orders which stands visually in front of the arch-series, throwing it back in space, as Palladio was to do more than a thousand years later in one of the most intellectual and sophisticated façade systems ever devised. This perhaps recondite arrangement can be seen in its unitary form on many
11 Roman triumphal arches, for example that of Titus in Rome. Here the screen of composite columns raised on a high base and carrying a vigorously projecting entablature seems to press back against the arch piers like a flattened portico, or one may say a peristyle since the columns surround the arch. It performs in fact
22 the same rôle as the pseudo-peripteral attached orders on a Roman temple, that of a vestigial colonnade: a little less than structure, for it honestly portrays its

dependence on the wall, yet a little more than decoration in its creation of a visual plane and its undoubted function (in temples and other places) as a buttress. In an arch like that of Titus the arch construction with its attic and heavy abutments seems to complete its statement behind (or within) the screen of columns. Where subtle visual analogies are uncalled for, as in the aqueducts, especially where the structure is appropriately or felicitously in rugged stone, the applied orders are not found. City bridges like the Mulvius had unpretentious stone ornament or aediculae between the arches on the cutwater piers, these latter sometimes acting as small sluice arches and therefore not primarily decorative in intention. In fact Roman decoration everywhere is either a gesture of urbanity wrestling with recalcitrant or inelegant materials, or it derives, sometimes analogously, from a structural form, in no case more gratuitous than, say, the decorative forms of a Greek Doric entablature.

Clearly the Romans had a taste for embellishment which was fostered in public building as an assertion of self-esteem which always accompanies prosperity and as an extension of imperial vanity and indulgence, but also, and in the first place, as a result of dressing the useful but unexpressive rubble and brick core, with its built-in flues and relieving arches, constructed without formal integration because it was always intended to be concealed by facing. It was to be many centuries before it began to be suggested that the brave show of architectural duplicity might be aesthetically immoral! With the development of this serviceable core material comes also the full realization of the almost infinite potential of brick, and the development of spatial complexity and structural clarity.

The architect has always been responsible for 'structuring' his buildings. He cannot be called an engineer in ancient Egypt because of the difficulty of handling granite and an artist in Greece because the stone he worked with lent itself to brilliance in sculptural ornament. We are asked to believe that he was an engineer in Roman times when he devised and handled sophisticated groin vaults and domes, but an architect (and an ostentatious and expendable one at that) when he caused them to be decorated. Curiously his position in the Middle Ages is ambiguous. One writer repudiates him as an engineer because he could not calculate mathematically in his structural designing; others cannot resist the ingenuity of stone construction stressed almost to the point of failure. All in all the evidence of form derived from structural manipulation is attractive to the engineer's image of himself. Altogether the apologists of the engineer have the best of it, and the architect is reduced to being a decorator of interiors or a formal designer in two dimensions of façades.

In all this, planning seems to be forgotten or considered not to be of very great importance in the analysis or assessment of a building. While it is true that

there are vast structures, like bridges, which seem to need little 'plan' consideration as such, and many others constructed according to traditional or 'routine'
plans, like aircraft hangars or basilican churches, yet drawing a plan is not like a
preparation for a game of hopscotch; the marks on a plan signify a thinking in
three dimensions, if not four; an awareness of the totality of the enclosure
anticipated, not simply what has been called the 'decorative part' of it.

This 'thinking back' found in some modern books on engineering is not truly
the history of engineering at all, but a scramble after ancestors for the portrait
galleries of an *arriviste* society. That is not to say that there are no ancestors,
but these are architects, and it would be more becoming, and better history, if
they were recognized as such. In fact we could do with some redefinitions and
newly orientated explorations in architectural history. Structural implications
have been too often neglected in stylistic analyses, but it should be clearly
understood that these structural implications are as much of architectural
significance as are the purely formal, and that in fact the purely formal in
architecture is of limited range, unless space-relations are considered purely
formal.

If there is one structure to which architect and engineer should agree to share
a historical claim it is, most appropriately, the bridge. Whether it was the
warrior or the hunter who first flung a tree across a gap, there is no break in the
continuous development of bridge construction for civil and military use. No
doubt it was the group of men detailed off to attend to the 'engines' of war who
would also be required to get the army across rivers and ravines; equally
certainly it was the architect who was required at home to provide the city
bridges and assure the constant supply of water that had to be brought across
the Campagna by aqueduct to Rome. Over the wide reaches of the Roman
empire some of the most marvellous structures of the three centuries after the
birth of Christ were aqueducts and bridges, and they were built, we must
suppose, by architects. Certainly as long as the stone bridge rested on arches,
either spanning the river in a single span or bracing its cutwaters against the
stream, it seems to have been taken for granted that the design lay in the hands
of architects. Only in the eighteenth century, with the establishment in France
first of the Department of Bridges and Roads, and then towards the middle of
the century of the *Ecole des Ponts et Chausées*, did the specialist emerge: the
civil engineer, who assured his place in the history of architecture with the first
bridge of cast iron, from which the architects of the day, to their shame, seem to
have shrunk in horror. At this time stone bridges were being constructed by
both architects and engineers. An architect, Robert Mylne had completed the
Blackfriars Bridge over the Thames in 1760 and fifty years later Telford built
his much-praised Waterloo Bridge, also in stone. 'Bridges are architecture,'

writes Elizabeth Mock, 'but architecture of a very special kind, unique in its single-mindedness.' She goes on to say:

> its reality lies not in space enclosed, but in structure itself. Since a bridge does not define space, but cuts through it, it is free of all the intricate psychological considerations that must be taken into account when space is moulded or enclosed. Thus, paradoxically, a bridge is at once the most tangible and most abstract of architectural problems. As such, it is capable of extraordinary purity, though it may perhaps never achieve the richness and depth of expression that are possible in buildings of more complex human motivation.[24]

What emerges from any study of modern bridges is that though they undoubtedly come into being through the creativity of the engineer (and perhaps more and more of the specialist engineer at that), he should not be disappointed to discover he has produced what must be called a work of architecture. There is no other name for it. 'Engineering' is an activity, not a collective name for artifacts. What is more, if we are going to allow that works of architecture may be works of art, then engineers as well as painters, sculptors, and architects are capable of designing and 'structuring' powerful works of art. All efficient bridges will not be so classified, but if we may name some that evoke a response that may be equated with that which modern sculpture or ancient temples may arouse we could suggest the concrete bridges of Maillart, suspension bridges like the Golden Gate bridge at San Francisco or the Brooklyn or Washington bridges in New York, and the Severn suspension bridge near Bristol, and trussed bridges in different parts of the world, of which one of the earliest to excite 'wonder and admiration' was the Firth of Forth bridge, completed in 1890.[25]

It was not only with the building of bridges, however, that the engineer led the way in nineteenth-century structures. Though some would deny him the title of engineer (and certainly that of architect), Joseph Paxton produced in 1851 what was to prove one of the most distinguished buildings of the century, the Crystal Palace. 'A greenhouse' Ruskin called it,[26] and in fact some large greenhouses built at the time (at Kew for example) were in themselves not entirely negligible. Apart from other structures of this genre, together with markets and like large places of assembly, there were the great railway stations like King's Cross and St. Lazare, and also docks, and lighthouses. It took a while for the architects to recognize, let alone follow, the lead they had been given, and even when they began to be aware of the possibilities of metal and reinforced concrete their first attempts at high-rise buildings show a totally unresolved compromise with design features which had developed from the use of stone and brick. Not many architects before Le Corbusier contributed to a

new aesthetic, and it continued to be the engineer who made progress in this as
well as structural advances in buildings of any considerable size. The famous
airship hangars at Orly were characteristically the work of an engineer,
Freyssinet.

Although Le Corbusier had advocated the emulation of modern engineering
design like that of cars, aircraft, and ships, he seems to have had a certain
reserve about the ability of engineers directly to produce architecture.[27] Le
Corbusier's criterion for making a work of art (as opposed merely to structural
skill) was the occurrence of 'passion' in its devising, and therefore presumably
in its apprehension. But one can surely not eliminate the possibility of this
emotional and emotive concomitant allied to advanced calculation, even if we
are prepared to concede that all constructive work does not bear witness to it.
The Egyptian pyramid has been the subject of repeated argument on this score.
Can a geometrically regular polyhedron be a work of art? No, say some, because
the 'hand' of the artist has no personal scope. Yes, say others, when it has been
conceived as the grave mound of a king and to a scale of a 760-foot side. Its
impressiveness may be partly environmental, but it is a product of human
imagination. So too, surely, is the fluency of a Maillart bridge.

Throughout the greater part of the nineteenth century the work of engineers
did not earn the praise it merited largely because they, like the architects and
most of the public, had become accustomed to the conventions of an aesthetic
orientation that made it all but impossible to regard the new materials and
structural developments as anything more than utilitarian, and visually repug-
nant or negligible. It was in fact the artists and architects, and not the engineers
themselves who were eventually to discern beauty in the new forms, and there
are probably more painters who have included the Eiffel Tower in their paintings of Paris than there have been engineers who have praised its beauty. It has
been pointed out by several writers that when engineers do become concerned
about the appearance of their works, they often make abysmal errors of judgement, not being properly trained to see where the beauty lies. This is, however,
surely not inevitably a permanent situation, and one may hope that a designer
capable of producing forms that others find admirable will ultimately be able to
admire them himself! It is true that the experienced viewer will recognize
felicitous relations where the less experienced person, or one less experienced in
contemporary aesthetics may not, and that the eloquence of imaginative mathematics may carry aesthetic implications not immediately perceptible to the
designer, but it would be presumptuous in the highest degree to assume therefore that a designer of the stature of Nervi does not know what he is doing, or
that Maillart did not realize what he had accomplished. There is no inevitably
'correct' way of designing structure, whether it be cover, span, or support,

4. The Severn Bridge, near Bristol

unless the structure is 'worked out' in terms of someone else's design. While therefore decision is referred to the engineer, we must concede aesthetic brilliance as well as mere competence, and especially, in such cases, as shells, vaults, and 'tents' which determine a whole character of vast buildings. In the preface to his *Aesthetics and Technology in Building* Nervi has written of 'a full and intrinsic agreement between aesthetic expression and the static and construction requirements or suggestions'. He goes on:

> The new materials, in particular reinforced concrete and steel, have form-giving possibilities, derived from their technological characteristics, that are completely different from those of wood or the masonry materials of the past. From these characteristics and from those intrinsic to the new themes brought about by our progressive social development, rather than from programmatic aesthetic tendencies (which act more efficiently when they enter the mind unconsciously), we can expect the directives and the suggestions for a new and grand architecture.[28]

For buildings they are, there is no getting away from that. A transfer of emphasis from enclosure to cover, from walls to vaults, from subdivided containers to open circulation area, does not remove from planner, designer, and builder the responsibility of providing a total environment. Certainly to see design as emanating wholly from calculation is somewhat to put the cart before the horse. There has to be an imaginative project before there can be a calculation. The hyperbolic paraboloid* does not in itself signify the end of the architect, but it is symptomatic of a change in emphasis in the kind of architecture that is needed now.

* Or saddle-shaped suspended roof, first used in Mexico by Felix Candela.

II

The Cave and the Crystal

The Cave and the Crystal represent two extremes of architectural character where the emphasis is wholly on either interior or exterior. Between these lies an infinite variety of container, cover, or support. Here we investigate some of the possibilities as shown by well-known buildings and building types. The analogies chosen are not meant to be pushed too far, and this section as a whole sets out to provide a provocative exercise in the analysis of architectural range and its aesthetic implications.

The Cave and the Crystal

There is not much evidence that the Cave Man (by which we usually mean man of the Old Stone Age) lived to any extent in caves. He took shelter in caves, but his nomadic life would doubtless have made it difficult to ensure a supply of suitable caves in the ebb and flow of his hunting expeditions, especially as his favourite quarry, the bison, must have preferred to graze on the plains. He might have dumped his family in a cave while he went foraging, using only the mouth, where there was light, but the use of the depths of the cave as a permanent residence seems unlikely.

In southern Africa, where much the same kind of life was evidently led by more recent hunter-artists, there are few habitable caves. The pictures that show where the people have been are painted on the underside and protected surfaces of rock ledges, or in fact incised on scattered stones: the people used portable tents made of hides, as they used light containers like gourds and ostrich eggs for their seeds and berries and scant water. Presumably Palaeolithic man was similarly equipped, though the inter-glacial climate even of southern France and Spain must have been considerably less inviting for camping out than the sunny reaches of the Kalahari.

However, that he made use of caves for purposes other than residential we do know, and perhaps our first consideration of significance is that the earliest use of shelter with which we are familiar is in fact not for the protection of man's person but for something infinitely less tangible. The pictures are certainly there, but the magic which they served can only be deduced or guessed at. The palimpsests that occur on all the sites that we know show that each act of magic was in itself temporary, to be superseded many times, but the place once chosen was permanent—perhaps the only permanence these people knew. Once the place had been consecrated it remained so, and was used for what, in this cultural epoch, we can only regard as a proto-religious activity.

There is no evidence that these caves were ever modified structurally. Not even the surfaces on which the drawings and paintings were made were in any way prepared. In caves like Altamira the very protuberances and irregularities formed part of the representations, which thus take on a quasi-relief character. In other caves, like Lascaux, the unevenness of the surface is simply ignored.

We cannot suppose caves had any less of an overawing effect on people of Palaeolithic times than they tend to have on us today. The silent darkness must have suggested their suitability for the preservation of magical marks quite as much as did the more practical aspect of protection from the elements. It should not surprise us then (though we may well be chastened by the revelation of the constancy of our emotional and spiritual equipment over the millennia) to find a great settled nation like the Egyptians giving an important rôle to excavation in providing places suitable for their religious activities. Tombs and temples were excavated, both in the ground and in the cliffs that follow the Nile River, and in this time of the emergence of great architecture we may read the influence of the cave.

6, p121

The cave is mysterious partly because of its darkness, but mainly because it is undefined externally, and therefore one cannot read from the outside either its shape or its extent. We talk of the 'mouth' of a cave, and this suggests that its only entrance will, as it were, swallow the intruder, whose further destiny is by this token unpredictable. We cannot know, from the outside, anything about the cave; the 'mouth' in no way defines the extent of the interior, which we assume expands, either in length or width or height, or all three. Now any way of building which provides this character of a cave has been called here 'excavation' architecture,[1] and we have a clear example in Egypt where actual excavation seems to have developed along with building of this type.

5   First of all there are the pyramid and the mastaba. The pyramid, usually solid in itself, covered an excavated tomb, often elaborate, consisting of corridors and chambers. The same sort of arrangement is found under the mastaba, though here we have the interesting situation that the system starts in the construction of the mastaba itself, where cavities in the masonry lead via shafts and corridors to the excavated chambers below.

The rock tombs and temples of the New Kingdom provide a similar complex of cavities bored into the face of the cliffs on the west bank of the river. The entrance was often undefined, deliberately concealed in the case of tombs, which were not to be disturbed after the funeral rites had been completed. Corridors with ramps or flights of steps led inwards and downwards, at intervals opening out into chambers of ritual significance with formally decorated walls, and sometimes treasure, and always the repetition of the image of the

5   6

deceased, ensuring his immortality, performing the same magical function of preservation and creation that was done by the drawings in the caves of Palaeolithic man. Apart from the 'mystery' conditioned by the internal arrangement's not being reflected, and therefore predicted, on the exterior of the building, there is an additional bewilderment produced by the building of cul-de-sac corridors and 'false' doors, intended to deter intruders whether mortal or supernatural.

Where the excavation in the rock was not meant to be concealed, emphasis could be given to the entrance, and this in some cases led to the hemi-speos, or 6, p121 half-cave. Here a constructed building extended the excavation outwards, so that the entrance might be vast and grand, gradually contracting and withdrawing to the 'mouth' of the smaller and darker area within the cliff itself. It is interesting that at about the time this type of hemi-speos was being built great Pylon temples were being raised on the opposite side of the river with a very p123 similar disposition of spaces to that of the speos or hemi-speos. After the unroofed but enclosed court comes the narrower covered hypostyle hall followed by the smaller and darker sanctuary, each zone smaller and more confined than the one before, with higher floor and lower ceiling, simulating the decreasing volumes of excavation. The placing of a simple very thick unpierced wall around the outside, concealing the inner structure, reduces the building to a solid mass into which the zones recede. Whether the temple follows the rock-excavations in time, or vice-versa, does not seem to have been established in this context, but that it emulates excavation can surely not be doubted.

Clearly the use of actual excavation to provide accommodation is limited, being promoted by geographical convenience as well as religious or even political motivation. Greek legend is dappled with references to caves in association with magical or religious matters: the birth of gods or the machinations of witches. This religious connection goes on through Roman times: catacombs, underground temples, such as the Basilica of Porta Maggiore in Rome, the crypt, which being often the heart of a martyrium remains the mysterious part of an early Christian church, silent, dark, and undefined. From time to time the cave—the excavation proper—appears. The Etruscan tombs were excavated in the volcanic matrix characteristic in the area of the Twelve Cities that formed the Etruscan Confederacy. The consistency of this—firmer than ordinary earth or clay, and less obdurate than ordinary rock—favoured the excavation technique which was used for the tomb itself, the location being sometimes marked by a tumulus, a pile heaped on a formal base, as at Cerveteri. The cutting away of the tufa did not stop at the mere provision of burial space, but rendered these spaces as though built, with supporting piers and 'beds' for the dead furnished with 'pillows', the whole decorated with painted reliefs realistically imitating

objects hanging on the walls: pots and pans, armour and clothing. Later
7 examples are at the strange rock-tombs of Petra, cut directly into the cliff face,
and finishing (or rather starting), with a late-antique façade also excavated from
the face of the rock.

This very sophisticated treatment directly links Petra and excavation generally with that type of 'excavated' building characteristic of seventeenth-
century architecture in Rome. The stimulus for this may be considered partly
topographical, for crowded and irregular sites often prevented buildings being
expressed externally, except in their upper parts. Still it is interesting that most
of these 'effects' are found again in religious buildings. The church with which
8 the tomb of El Khasne at Petra has been directly compared is San Carlo alle
Quattro Fontane, whose façade appears to echo it, but one wonders how clearly
Borromini conceived that he was following the idea of a cave in far more than
just this. The available site appears, in fact, so blocked in, and so irregular that
the architect had no recourse but to initiate his building as the inside of a shell.
We have his serial drawings, but in each case, having established his axes, he
manoeuvres the plan of this quite small church as a series of geometrical forms,
especially tangential circles. Having made his final decision about the inside
skin with its symmetrical chapel entrances, he then simply blocks in the rest
back to the boundary lines. Not quite, though, for there is the west front
communicating with the street. This is by no means simply the outside of the
west end of the nave. Here he designed a façade, like Petra's to be imposed as
though it were a cliff face, upon the outside wall, with the difference that upon
it ripples the wave and swell hinting at the undulations within. A dome completes the effect of enclosure in the church, and here light is permitted to
enter—the vault of a cave penetrated by fissures from the earth's surface.

All of Borromini's churches in Rome have something of this quality. Sant'
Agnese provides the sense of expansion beyond the scope of the façade, while
Sant'Ivo, being centralized, has the continuity of total enclosure. The technique
is not, of course, peculiar to Borromini. The 'topographical' situation applies in
most churches of the time, and the emotionally charged directive of counter-
Reformation art, inevitably turning inward upon the worshipper makes interiors
doubly overwhelming. Santa Maria in Vallicella in Rome by Martino Longhi
shows this strong character of planning from within. The constant sliding in
and out of the side walls, alternately confining and releasing the visitor, eventually presents him with the swinging continuity of the domed centre. On plan
can also be seen the echo, or foreboding, of this in the broken and vacillating
façade.

This parietal Baroque planning does not apply only to buildings whose outer
walls are confined. Something like the technique used in the Egyptian temple,

of disposing the internal surfaces and effects, and then setting them within the
heavy agglutinate of the outside walls, tends to prevail. If the plan of a Baroque
church is studied it will be noted that the shape of the piers results, not from an
inner to outer structural necessity (as in the case of a Gothic cluster pier) but 51
from the shape desired for the interior of a zone, as a seal reflects the negative of
the desired stamp.[2]

Excavation architecture is thus the designing of a space, and it is the space
that should be read on the plan rather than the solids, which are merely its
boundaries. The masonry is in fact the matrix out of which the space has been
'carved'. This does not mean that the masonry has no substance. The existence
of a cavity implies comparatively massive surroundings, or at least massive
enough to withstand the inroads made upon it by the cavity as they are in
Byzantine churches. To compensate for these are the solid parts that result
when two or more cavities adjoin. This way of designing continues after the
seventeenth century, and Robert Adam's round and oval rooms *en suite* afford p143
an elegant example from the eighteenth century. The party wall of London
houses is but another instance of a confining topography.

In complete contrast to the spatial intentions of the cave, the crystal presents
itself to us as a solid body with several faces or facets. It is usually in fact a
polyhedron, though for our purposes we may consider it as any solid geometrical figure, as a cylinder, a cone, even a sphere, or a part or a compound of
these figures. Its essential characteristics are that it is solid, and that the surfaces
we are aware of define its bulk and extent, and do not in any way refer to
interior spaces. It is a structure in its architectural exemplar, and not a mono-
lith, and can thus, and by this means, usually be distinguished from sculpture.
For, not being to any great extent a container or a shelter, it seems usually to

7   8   9

5 serve the purpose of a monument, and thus to some extent shares the propensities of sculpture. It is perfectly represented by the Egyptian pyramid.

Now the plan of a pyramid in itself is merely an opaque square. The Great Pyramid of Cheops (or Khufu) does contain some buried passages and chambers, but this is unusual, and the characteristic pyramid is a solid heap of masonry taking on a regular geometrical form, which is perfected by being faced with a series of blocks wrought from a finer stone, immaculately jointed and polished to an unbroken surface.

The pyramid is a grave mound. It is a stopper over the tomb of such weight and dimensions as to close and define it for ever. This great size, almost beyond appraisable scale, is directly responsible for its effect. If it were reduced to a size at which for instance it could be regarded as a desk ornament it would become, in fact, what it has often been called, 'merely' a simple geometric form. At the size at which it has actually been made, the austerity of its design is the factor that renders it evocative of wonder and terror, making it a powerful piece of architecture. It is not seen isolated in uncharted desert but in a set of relations which make it more assessible. On plan the full implications of these relations are clear: the pyramid is tied to the river by the decisive band of the causeway linking the two temples, the river temple, which receives, holds, and then sets the visitor on to the causeway and the pyramid chapel to which he is carried across the desert, and which defines his journey's end at the implacable slopes of the pyramid itself. Here at the base, over 750 feet long, the pyramid might well appear to him totally undefinable. The walls of all Egyptian buildings have a quickening vertical perspective increasing their apparent height, owing to the batter with which they were usually built.* But the pyramids had a slope of 50°, which at close quarters must have sent the apex shooting upwards, to dissolve at an incalculable point in the dazzling sky.

I have made some reference to the burrowings in the pyramid of Cheops, and it does so happen that the buildings which exemplify the crystal may often be taken also as examples of the cave. Provided the cavities remain unassociated with the outer surfaces the two characters are natural counterparts of each other. This is immediately observable in the case of the mastaba, which serves much the same purpose as the pyramid on a less spectacular scale, and it even applies to a certain extent to the temples, both of the pylon type and of the p120 earlier and simpler form found in the Pyramid Complex, where the plan shows a massive solid block of masonry 'burrowed' into by passages and chambers of shape and size nowhere related to the outer surfaces—one cannot say of the walls, since these are not walls as such.

---

* That is to say, one face of a wall inclined inwards from the vertical.

In deciding then which buildings may be regarded as 'crystalline'* we may consider those which have no demonstrable relationship between interior and exterior, and have therefore been shaped without regard to their containing function. That these must be monuments of some sort seems inevitable. An isolated example of the crystal is perhaps the small choragic monument of Lysicrates, in Athens, which, though it may contain an inside chamber, is a 9 building of purely external significance. Here we have a basically cylindrical form with attached columns and a decorative superstructure placed upon a solid or solid-appearing plinth. This consideration of moulded or decorated surfaces of massive solid structure turns one's mind to the type of a triumphal arch, 11 which certainly possesses some of the characteristics of a crystalline building. The essence of this type of structure is its solidity and its outward-facing genre, which cause it to invade the space around it and dominate its surroundings. The plan of a monument means nothing, except in its setting, in relation to other buildings. It marks a place and gives its own meaning to it.

If we turn from the pyramids to monumental tombs of later times, we find the mausoleums of Halicarnassos, Augustus, and Hadrian in Rome and Theodoric in Ravenna, all rather lumpish and on the whole unappealing buildings, with little of the assertive purity of the pyramid. It must be faced that an ambition for the grand often leads to the grandiose, and if we glance (briefly) at the monument in Rome to Victor Emmanuel II, designed in 1884, we shall see how far the building with no function except to commemorate can lead us away from architecture.

Since large-scale sculpture can so happily be used for monuments and, combined with some architectural support like fountain structures, provide all that city or parklands might need for focal points or visual emphases, the crystalline

---

* The word as used here makes no reference to material; it does not imply translucency or partial transparency.

type of building seems almost always referred to some sort of shrine. In this guise, where its containing rôle is of minimal complexity and maximum significance, probably the most splendid type of crystal ever produced by architects is 10, 23 the Greek Doric temple.

The term 'crystalline'* has in fact been associated with the peripteral temple many times, the implication being that it can be seen as a complete statement and that the proper view of it is the external. For this reason it must be considered in this section, though it is referred to later in a different context.

The housing of a cult statue and gifts brought in its honour is a simple function requiring only an adequate chamber with an access door as the sole communication with the exterior. If therefore the designers wished to draw attention to the structure they were free to set it and dress it at will. From early times the Greek architects elected to surround their larger and more important shrines with a peristyle supporting the roof, which covered the sanctuary and projected all around to rest on an entablature. The peristyle is thus structurally a covered terrace, or walkway, around the central structure, and to this extent a simple extension to the primary enclosure. The very intercolumniations may seem to invite penetration to the interior.

Passing between them, however, does not, except at the ends, lead to the interior, and the hard blankness of the naos wall is evident from quite a distance away. Even at the ends, there is often at one end no door, and at the other a door set behind further columns, and not necessarily open to all at all times. The ceremonial altar is certainly outside the peristyle, and the covered colonnade can perhaps more easily be seen as an outward-facing than as an inward-indicating system. The peristyle may be seen thus as containing or distancing the shrine. It is really only after accepting the impenetrability of the peristyle that one can accept the crystalline quality of the temple.

It would, however, be wayward indeed not to do so. For probably not in the whole history of architecture has there been a building that has promoted, and continued to promote, so much admiring regard for its external effects, whether from a distance or from close by, together with less concern about the interior. It has been thought that this concern with the externalizing, or crystalline, view of the temple is an old one, and that the ancient Greek, slowly approaching it, whether along a formal route within the temenos, or up the winding way of a sacred hill, never intended to penetrate the interior, nor to do more than join the celebrants at the outside altar. The temple turned gradually as he approached, presenting illimitability of columned flank, or majesty of fully pedimented end, as his path wound by. When he was upon it, it was almost too

* But here the word has usually connoted something of transparency and sparkle.

big for him to see, but its shining totality had been suggested to him on the way.[3]

The departures from geometrical regularity in the Doric temple are well known, but they are interpreted differently by different scholars. The canonical Doric temple has a portico of six columns at each end and in the mature temple this results in a variety in spacing between the outer pairs of columns, the inner pairs, and the central pair which are the furthest apart. The lintel proper is the architrave, plain in the Doric order and, of course, not one continuous length of stone but a piece between each pair of columns finely joined to the next piece. The spacing of the columns necessarily allows for the steady bearing of their own weight and that of the superstructure and a convenient size of architrave block. Above the architrave is the Doric frieze of alternate triglyph and metope, each a separate stone and therefore presenting several joints to be borne by the architrave. Traditionally the frieze starts with a triglyph at each end and bears a triglyph in the centre of the portico, and above the centre of each column, so that as the triglyphs are a regular width, each metope must needs vary slightly in size from its neighbours.

None of these variations is immediately noticeable. The whole peristyle has a slight inward batter, and this in spite of the fact that it stands on a base sloping outwards, as the stylobate rises in the centre like a mound, whether, as some say, to counteract the optical or actual effect of sinking, or for the more prosaic but very practical purpose of throwing off rainwater. Probably few of these subtle irregularities are visible to the passing or approaching spectator. The entasis of the columns, however, often is, especially in the earlier temples where it is sometimes very pronounced. It would seem that the greater warmth of animate curves is preferred to rigid geometrical profiles and it is also possible that the masons wished to provide a vertical thrust for the base of the column, desirable in the Doric order which rests without a footing on the stylobate.

The peripteral temple has come to be accepted as the epitome of fine architecture, though it is questionable whether all of those who do accept this could give reasons why it should be so regarded. Certainly it has something to do with simplicity, standardization, craftsmanship, and a sensibility to relations which promoted a delicate and continuous adjustment of these as time went on, so that the building was always alive and spoke precisely of its time.

Tunnel and Tube

A tunnel differs from a cave in having an opening at each end. It is fundamentally a burrow, with an internal expression only, while a tube (which is therefore a form of box) has an exterior surface which lies parallel to that of the interior. Its use in this pure form is limited architecturally to galleries, covered passageways, very large drainpipes and sewers like the famous Cloaca Maxima of the Romans, temporary shelters, and (if one may include these) vehicles such as certain kinds of trains or trailers, aircraft, and underwater structures and ships.

What we must classify as a tunnel, however, is our old friend the tunnel or barrel vault, and the structures it helps to create. It is seldom reflected externally, and this relates it to other 'excavated' architecture. This is particularly applicable to medieval churches in southern France in which the vault construction is so heavy that it cannot always carry clerestory windows: well-known examples are at Poitiers in Anjou, Clermont-Ferrand in Auvergne, or Conques or Toulouse to the south-west. We might even include Sant'Ambrogio in Milan because its early cross-vault is so heavy and laborious that it appears as an excavation rather than a canopy.

Less arduous tunnels are those of sixteenth-century churches in Italy: Sant'Andrea in Mantua, Il Gésu and its followers in Rome. They all have the regularity of progression that characterizes the true tunnel. So do they also have two ends, one at the entrance (and sometimes indicated on the façade, as at Sant'Andrea) and one at the crossing, where the tunnel gives way to the dome. It is a far more logical approach to the dome than a flat or coffered ceiling, for it should provide one of the four arches that form the pendentives. This is done very meticulously in Sant'Andrea, as are all the internal–external relations. Alberti unfortunately did not live to see its completion and tackle the upper portion himself, which is the only part not thoroughly resolved. From a scrutiny of the transept façade it would appear that the intention might have been a high pedimental slope over the oculus into the upper part of the nave, as was to be done later by Palladio in his Venetian churches. Obviously the greater height of a barrel-vaulted nave was presenting Alberti with a new problem.

No architect, even Alberti, could do anything about the fact that the vault or ceiling of a long nave obscures the dome. At Santa Maria delle Grazie in Milan, Bramante appears to have been thoroughly impatient with the existing medieval building, and has apparently made no attempt to weld his new part to the old (as Alberti so painstakingly did at Santa Maria Novella in Florence). In fact he has distorted the last bay of the vault in order to get his arch-approach to the crossing to the height he desired. This difficulty is evidently one reason why they all tended to prefer the shorter arms of the Greek cross, or the centralized plan defined by the dome itself. This applies only to architects after the Humanist revival. During the Middle Ages the attitude was a bit different, though the gradual but persistent evolution of 'gothic space' indicates that Romanesque solutions were not quite complacently accepted.

The characteristic of the French eleventh-century church, say Sainte Foy at Conques, was the clarity and naïveté with which the various parts of the church were assembled: first, the sturdy western towers (late at Conques but raised on the early foundations) which defined the entrance block; then the nave, a narrow dark tunnel despite its height, propped up by side aisles with tribune galleries over. These admitted some light which did not penetrate sufficiently to the nave to modify its burrow-like character. Abruptly the nave ends at the crossing, where, hoisted above squinches, a lantern admits bright light. The east end with ambulatory and radiating chapels is not really a continuation of the nave, though the heavy construction throughout prevents everywhere any sense of communication with air, light or space outside. It has been demonstrated that High Gothic cathedrals, like Reims and Amiens, have the quite opposite effect: that continuity of mouldings, and diagonality of set, fold the structure outward like a lip, provide the smooth passage of space between exterior and interior,* and by the same token free the movement of space within the zones of the cathedral. No longer is there an abrupt transition from nave to crossing. The tunnel vault has been replaced by the network of ribs that do not form a continuous surface, and the dome, the suspended beehive, has made way for the broken surface of the crossing vault which in no way imposes itself as a separate and positive entity.

* But see also p. 87.

12   13   14

The Post and the Pit

The post is a building whose salient characteristic is to have only one important dimension, height. This is apparent at once in its plan, which has no extension in any direction, and may, in its extreme form, appear as little more than a dot. Any monumental column—like those, for instance, of Trajan or Marcus Aurelius in Rome, or even more extreme, the columns in Venice bearing the signs of St. Mark and St. Theodore—are of this nature, but we may consider more substantial buildings, like towers, as examples of this genre. Occasionally the single post or tower serves as a vertical marker to a horizontal termination (and in this plays the rôle of monument to some extent and may be identified with the crystal), but it is more usually, and perhaps more properly, intended to serve its obvious function, that of achieving height. This being so any interior space it may possess is purely an adjunct to its principal purpose, which is to be seen, or to see from. A beacon, a bell tower, or a lighthouse serve the first purpose, a watch tower or a lookout, the second. Very often the hollow interior is given over entirely to a means of ascent: a spiral staircase, or a lift in modern towers.

Bell towers or belfries served the double purpose of raising the bells to a height from which their tolling would be effectively heard, and then of guiding the people towards the church itself. The early Christian churches in Italy had campanili which stood independently of the church they served, and could be round or square in plan. The usual method of building a brick tower was to make it appear solid at the base with an increasing number of arched openings on each level as it rose. This both lightened the actual structure of the upper parts and provided an open area at the highest part, where the bells were hung, to carry the sound across the surrounding area. These towers could be extremely elaborate, like the cylindrical tower at Pisa, with six platforms with marble arcading, and two more open to the sky. This is a heavy stone tower of 52 foot diameter, whose foundations have sunk unevenly into the earth causing the famous and now dangerous tilt. The so-called 'Lily Tower' of Florence Cathedral is reputed to have been the work of Giotto. It is a square of 45 feet, and was encrusted with sculptures of leading Florentine artists, most of which have been removed to safer repositories.

Watch-towers too usually date from the Middle Ages, when they formed an important part of both public and private defence. Elegant examples are those of the Palazzo Vecchio in Florence and the Palazzo Pubblico in Siena, with their ornate but business-like crenellations, while whole towns showed a competitive spirit, like Bologna and San Gimignano, each great family trying to outdo the next in the height of towers attached to their urban residences. An architec-

turally interesting development in Venice has occurred where later churches
imitated the great tower in the Piazza S. Marco, thus presenting similar ver- 57
sions of the square tower with its arcaded open platform for the bells and steep
pyramidal spire.

Belfries were incorporated into the medieval cathedrals of France and
England, and appear in the form of portal towers on the continent and usually
crossing towers in England. The famous spires of Wren's churches were most 17
effective in indicating the situation of the various parish churches in the dense
complexity of the City of London. His way of emphasizing height was to build
in diminishing layers, like a telescope, until the summit was reached.

There is a sort of excitement in towers, the exhilaration of an identification
with sheer height, which is perhaps nowhere more keenly felt than at the Eiffel 41
Tower in Paris, whether one is standing below incredulously staring at the web
of metal soaring upwards, or actually at the top looking in enchantment at the
city of Paris stretching into the distance. Here is a 'post' whose only purpose
was height. Higher structures there may be today, but surely none more telling.

One of the most appealing and 'romantic' types of tower is the lighthouse.
The earliest one we know of was the Pharos of Alexandria which has given its
name in several languages to that type of structure. It was built in the third
century B.C. and was considered one of the Seven Wonders of the World in
ancient times. A 'pharos' was also built at Dover by the Romans, but the first

15   16   17

lighthouse of modern times off the English coast was the Eddystone Lighthouse, built by Henry Winstanley, and first lit (by candles!) in November 1698. It was destroyed and rebuilt several times, the present one dating from 1882.

Very few lighthouses seem to have been built since the middle of the twentieth century, and of these by far the most interesting are those which have virtually dispensed with the traditional 'tower' shape, and incorporate modern mechanisms for raising equipment and for the lighting itself. Those with architectural 'pretensions' (like the Columbus lighthouse chosen as the result of a competition held in 1930) are often aesthetically unacceptable. The 'new' lighthouse at Dungeness built in 1960, is an elegant version of more or less traditional form. A cylinder rests on a spiral ramp to a public platform, while a splayed top draws attention to the lighting and foghorn equipment.

Perhaps the lighthouse reached its high moment at the turn of the century, and is something of an anachronism in these days of radar and other advanced methods of communication. This may be why the traditional shape with its graceful convex sides and domical top seems to us the most moving. A tower designed for radio transmission will evoke no such nostalgic yearnings, though chimneys of potteries and even factories may.

If the post suggests height, the pit characteristically suggests depth. It is clearly a form of excavation, literally. It is in fact a hole, a hole lined in most cases with masonry: a well, a grave, a cesspool, an approach route to the Cthonic gods, a sinking for a mine, a storage bin.

Though in a structural sense somewhat negative, the idea of a pit can carry strong emotional associations, particularly in its implications of burial and imprisonment, and its long relationship with the early gods of the earth and underworld. Any grave involving interment is a form of pit, and for these we can turn to innumerable historic and modern types. The shaft under an Egyptian mastaba, finely lined, is a type which ranks as formal architecture; the casual hole in the turf is of course not. The Pit, as against the Cave or Tunnel, implies a vertical sinking, though it may afterwards be closed or covered, for safety, or for protection of whatever the pit contains. Because a pit cannot be seen from a distance, it is usually, whatever its purpose, given some marker, and this can become an important extension architecturally. Notably here we think of wells, whose heads, combining the marker function with that of providing a mechanism for drawing water, have found many expressions varying from vernacular forthrightness to formal sculpture. Perhaps we can associate with the well any pit containing water: springs and pools that have been given a formal setting, reservoirs and swimming baths. In the ancient world the cistern was an important provision for water in time of drought or siege. Not so much a pit in appearance, as an underground tank or cellar often of considerable dimensions, it nevertheless falls into the group of excavation which is a hole or hollow rather than a burrow. In Roman and early Christian or Byzantine times (for instance at Istanbul) cisterns were built in the form almost of hypostyle halls with regularly disposed columns, sunk deep in the mud of the reservoir bottom, and at the top supporting capitals bearing cupolas or vaults which carry the floors of buildings above. Dry and wet docks are pits that are part excavation and part structure, so is any container of produce or living fish or animals.

We should explain 'sunken' in terms of the way we have regarded the other categories, as having a 'sunken' character. It is conceivable that a 'pit' could be created on the top of a skyscraper. A building like a gas or water tower, however, is a 'box', for its external walls reflect its internal volume. A pit has no external walling!

The Box and the Cage

Most buildings are boxes. Boxes are containers in which the inner and outer surfaces are the two 'sides' of the fabric that form the box. There is thus a maximum amount of enclosed space for the volume occupied by the structure as a whole. This internal space may be subdivided both horizontally and vertically by partitions which again displace as little volume as possible. Boxes and their internal partitioning are usually rectangular in plan and elevation, but not necessarily so. They may be cylindrical (like a pill-box or a pillar-box) or ₂ polygonal-sided (like a stud-box) or in fact any convenient geometrical form or combinations of forms, but in every case the interior shape may be deduced from the external appearance, and the partitioning system is easily read on the plan or plans, and sometimes on the elevations.

Buildings that are boxes may have the planes that define their boundaries pierced to form openings, and these openings may be glazed, or contain doorways, or a whole plane may be made of glass, as it may be made of brick or concrete or timber. A row of buildings may be a continuous series of boxes juxtaposed, sharing their dividing walls. Or a building may be formed of a group of boxes of different shapes and sizes.

Like the boxes whose character they share the buildings may vary considerably in arrangement and treatment. They may be grand and formal, utilitarian, drab, or dour, bizarre, affected, absurd. When we call them good we usually mean that we find them simple, well-defined, and well-proportioned, going about their business directly of containing what they are meant to contain.

Changes of style reflect changes of taste and do not really affect buildings as much as is often thought. The sobriety and adaptability of a Georgian town house is not really so different from a domestic unit designed today for the same site and serving the same functions. Fewer partitions no more affect the box-character than smaller families change human nature. If we assume equally adept planning and sensitivity to detail and relations, then a change of style, like a change of fashion, becomes chiefly a change of emphasis.

The introduction of the so-called 'free' plan in the early decades of this century did have an effect on architecture, though in some respects one not as far-reaching as might have been anticipated. While urban control continued to offer the prospective builder the same kind of portion of chopped-up land, and the same planning and building restrictions, and taking into account building materials available in relation to economic considerations, there could not be, and has not been, a great deal of change. Building is still a matter of enclosure, and the most economic way to achieve this is by means of a box or group of boxes, the simplest and most curtailed outer surface remaining in general the cheapest. The free-plan has therefore been more popular as a means of sub-division than of basic layout. This changes the flavour of interiors whose more informal disposition is reflected by the asymmetry of façade arrangements. Where the change seems to be more fundamental than this it may well be that some structure-type other than the box is involved, and this may well be, in the 22, 29 first place, the Cage, which will be discussed presently.

As the box is, on the whole, the most economical kind of structure it is widely used for domestic building. Apart from vernacular and off-the-peg or stereo-type buildings (considered elsewhere) we shall find distinguished examples of the box in all periods and zones of habitation since very early times. The plan of an Egyptian house, usually single-storeyed and with a flat roof, shows at an early stage the feeling for easy transitions from confined to expanded spaces that is characteristic of imaginative and competent planning. The Great Hall of the Tudor house (a zoned box) giving way slowly to the subdivided gaunt carcass of the Elizabethan Great House does not forfeit its generous enclosing character.

18   19

How adequate and beautiful this simple, almost mathematical process of subdivision can render the internal parts of the house may be seen in the splendid
rooms of Hardwick Hall, for we seem to be endowed with a special sense of 18
response to noble spaces. Mathematical relations may indeed have something
directly to do with it. Architects seem frequently to have thought so, notably
the classic-minded Inigo with his double- and single-cubed rooms at Wilton
and the grand cube in the Queen's House, referred to earlier. These mathe- 19
matically related proportions of the Renaissance Humanist may not be read in
the plan alone; the elevation becomes relevant here. Though of course the
precision and obsessional mathematics of, for instance, Palladio's plans themselves imply elevations closely related to these plans.

The charming Georgian box has already been mentioned. Tall and narrow,
its elevations are fully implied in the ingenuity of its plan and the salient placing
of the stairs. A Robert Adam could convert the box partly into a cave, using the p143
enclosure resulting from the use of party walls as a basis for turning the rooms,
or some of them, inwards upon themselves. Otherwise they maintain the limpid
tranquillity of facing forward and back, and involving roof lighting for the well
of the stairs. These houses give a special meaning to the word 'urbane' and
never become obsolete, in spite of an almost total change in social relations since
they were built. The fact that not all can afford them does not alter their
architectural propriety and their continued comfort and convenience for living.

The more immediately practical apartment house is after all only a box whose 35
subdivisions represent repetitions of the domestic unit rather than extensions to
it. The controversial divided boxes, or multiple-assemblage boxes, of Le
Corbusier define more clearly than most their structural and functional nature.
Characteristically this is implicit in the plan. On the ground, simply the *pilotis*,
the stand upon which the total box must be lifted if the lowest floor is to have 20, p147
the same quality as any other.* At the level of that floor the plan gives the key
to the unit subdivision of the whole building.

The box provides an enclosure. The cage confines without enclosing visually.
It offers limitation to both ingress and egress. The structure supports itself by
means of its spaced ribs or framed sections, and not, as in the case of the box,
by means of the continuous vertical walls that form its delimiting surfaces. In a
very real sense a window cages an area, since except in relatively small areas the
glass is supported in the framework of the glazing system. We should probably
not apply this classification to that traditional type of window that is virtually
just a pierced hole in a wall, but where the window in any sense replaces a wall,
we have the example of a structure partaking at least of the character of a cage.

* See also p. 81.

It will be seen that this applies to a great deal of building of this century, especially in clement latitudes, where visual and actual continuity of interior 21, p149 and exterior space are fostered. Buildings associated with the historic Bauhaus may be examined in this context. The 'glass houses' of Mies van der Rohe and his followers, the work of Gropius and Neutra in America, and of course the p146 *oeuvre* of Le Corbusier provide distinguished examples.

At this point we may note something of interest. As we look at plans of buildings which have anything of the 'cage' quality we often find that they are framed structures in themselves, this being achieved either by containing supporting members at intervals within the surrounding skin, or by piers set within the area defined by the plan, acting as supports for the horizontal layers of the buildings, like the layers of a cake-rack or *compotier*. The glass skyscraper envisaged by Mies van der Rohe would be of this genre. Practically speaking it would be possible to make all the external 'walls' of a structure of either of the types defined above of glass, or indeed to have no walls at all. Functionally, however, this openness or transparency is not always desirable, and opaque screens are introduced, sometimes with smaller windows pierced in them. Structurally where such walls are not fundamentally load-bearing we may regard buildings of this type as falling under the 'cage' classification.

Now although we may not be able always to recognize this from the face of a building, which may be finished in such a way as to conceal its framed structure, it is almost always clear from the plan. Professor Michelis in his penetrating analysis of the difference between the Byzantine and Classical wall,[4] showed that the former was a randomly pierced surface, while the latter obeyed the fundamental demand of the framed structure in that its windows could fall only between supporting piers and were therefore characterized by regularity and superposition.

It is within the classical repertoire too that a subtle inversion of the cage structure arose, and that was the extension of the load-system of wall and pier

20   21

to include the colonnaded exterior. For here we have the physical possibility of passage between the columns, but a visual definition of a covered area. The continuity of the colonnade suggests a surface, comparable with the 'surface' of a cage. Clearly the cage and the box work together, extending each other's functional and architectural versatilities. A Greek temple is a box within a cage; a portico may be a cage attached to a box. More subtle combinations present themselves in contemporary design, where various kinds of spatial interpenetration have been contrived.

10

22, 29, 30

Domestic buildings have no sort of prerogative here, for this kind of building clearly lends itself to conditions of exposure suitable to specific settings which may differ greatly. The greenhouse, for instance, large or small, is a cage condition, or the orangerie, which performs a not dissimilar function. The unique extreme case of the Crystal Palace, but also the very many pavilions and roofed galleries, not to mention railway stations of the last century, used the combination of glass and cast iron to provide a maximum of both enclosure and daylight. It is the same constructive intention that protects canaries from hawks or plants from the elements, while ensuring the maximum sense of freedom compatible with this intention.

Before we turn away from the subject of box-type structures we should spend a moment on the Casket. A casket is a special sort of box meant to hold something precious, and it partakes of the preciousness by an elaboration of treatment. It is often lined internally or ornamented externally in such a way that its outer surfaces (including the lid) do not at all reveal the precise shape nor the actual size of the interior, nor the sometimes varying thicknesses of the material of which it is made. It is not without significance that a coffin is referred to as a 'casket', for men have held through the ages a very reverent attitude to the remains of people important to them, and one would expect a casket-type of building to be often related to a tomb or a shrine.

22

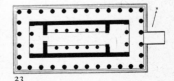

23

24   La Sainte Chapelle, in the precincts of the old royal palace on the Ile de la
Cité in Paris, has been likened to a jewel box, although it has also more properly
been called a reliquary (which is also a casket) since it was built to contain a
fragment of the Crown of Thorns brought to France by St. Louis (Louis IX).
Like most proper caskets it stands on a base (the crypt) the main floor being
reached by little staircases in the corners. The approach from the palace was by
way of an open gallery or loggia on the main floor level. Above the dimly lit
crypt is the brilliantly coloured main area of the chapel, the source of this
brilliance being both the stained glass windows that form the greater part of the
walls, and the gilding and decoration on the solid parts of the interior including
the vault, which is blue with gold stars. Here the precious relic was housed.

It is not easy to see this chapel externally, as it is so hemmed-in by later
buildings, but it is of characteristic thirteenth-century stone construction,
which does not reveal the details of the interior, though it does suggest the
single larger volume upon its lower base. Other royal chapels have somewhat of
this casket-like character, though perhaps no other shows a like adornment.
That of Windsor Castle, and King's College Chapel at Cambridge, are larger,
airier examples. If we go back in time the tomb of Galla Placidia in Ravenna is a
charming casket, and there are many such in the early Christian and Byzantine
world. The church of the monastery at Daphni, the little churches of Athens,
including the old Metropolis, are among examples too numerous to list. Santa
Costanza, the tomb said to have been built for Constantine's daughter, is a
circular casket with a central dome ringed by an ambulatory whose barrel-
vaulted ceiling has a mosaic of vine-patterns, and motifs of purely pagan derivation.

This circular building introduces the thought of those many examples of
Tholos erected by both Greeks and Romans. The usual arrangement was a
cylinder surrounded by a peristyle, and therefore perhaps qualifying for a 'box-
and-cage' hybrid. But when they are small, as this type usually is, they have a
precious treatment which makes them essentially 'caskets'. And perhaps in fact
we should extend the classification, not only to the many little temples and
treasuries, prostyle or *in antis*, such as line the Sacred Way to the Oracle at
Delphi, or abound like booths outside the stadium at Olympia, but even to
include the large and stately peripteral temples themselves.* For, from this
point of view, what is the Parthenon, of translucent marble fastidiously carved
and set on its formal base, somewhat removed in scale and bearing from the
human passer-by, but a finely wrought container for the statue of the goddess,
as in fact all the great temples, Olympia, Sunium, Aegina, were for the

* See also above p. 60.

Olympian gods and goddesses. What we have said about Greek temples applies too to Roman which were largely based on the Greek in appearance and intention.

At the turn of the fifteenth century architects and artists must have felt themselves very close to the intellectual spirit of their forbears, perhaps nowhere more than in Rome itself. There seems in fact to have been a surge forward at this time to re-establish life on the social level of the best of the world of antiquity, and, although the great days of excavation and reinterpretation were still to come, enough vigour and creativity emerged to cause historians of a later day to consider it in fact the 'high' renaissance of classicism. It was during these early years of the sixteenth century that Michelangelo established himself in Rome, that Raphael began to respond to the patronage of Julius II, and that Bramante became known as the architect with the most 'Roman' hand of them all.

His Tempietto in the cloisters of S. Pietro in Montorio was built in 1502, and 25 its very nickname indicates its character, which is that of a little Roman temple. It is only about 15 feet in its inner diameter, and, except for a small crypt below ground, is a simple cylinder covered with a dome and surrounded by a peristyle on ground level supported on a low plinth. A succession of critics has expressed itself as delighted with the Roman character of the little church built over the reputed site of St. Peter's martyrdom, and serving thus as a *martyrium*. It conforms to Alberti's desiderata for a temple, and to the less specific dicta of Vitruvius. Nevertheless the 'Roman' flavour is here elusive, and perhaps not entirely demonstrable, first because of a certain elaborateness in the detailing of the plan, and second because of the manner of the building itself. Antiquity carries a certain simplicity not quite evident here; it is perhaps unlikely that

24   25   26

such an elaborate dome would be found on such a small temple. Later planning is a little more tight than that of antiquity, and Roman examples seem to be higher and more removed from the directly human scale. This is very characteristically a casket of the Italian Renaissance.

The Hive and the Honeycomb

The beehive shape is of course not designed by bees but by man, and it is interesting that he should have given them for their shelter one of the earliest forms that he had devised for his own. Made as it often has been of perishable material it is impossible to reconstruct its historical origins, but it is fair to assume they were very early, since we find it in use today among people living in the simplest situations. It is used, as everyone knows, by the Eskimos, where its form is the only conceivable one to be devised from packed ice or snow, and 27 it is the traditional shape of hut to be fashioned by the Zulu and Swazi people, so far away, in such a different material that the similarity must be considered either coincidental or dependent on something almost as natural to men as its nest is to a bird.

The Zulu hut is woven of branches, withies, and grass reeds, and is made like a huge basket, the heavier branches plunged into the ground to define the domed form, and the smaller then woven across them, usually in a positive and even elaborate pattern. Both this and the igloo have one low-arched entrance, low both to exclude weather and to reduce any visitor to a vulnerable position. One could imagine other shapes in basket work though none more logical than this. The round takes precedence over the rectangular in fabrication, as far as we can see, and the gourd and the ostrich egg are imitated in clay and in the extremely fine basket work used for grain winnowers, beerstrainers, and hats.

The basket itself may be considered as a kind of box, cylindrical or rectangular, used for dwellings and often set in what have been called 'free-form' enclosures. In the ancient history of the West the beehive appears in Achaea, as a tomb, the dome being arrived at inevitably by corbelling on a circular plan. This is a true beehive shape (which the first two examples were not, being more nearly hemispherical) and rises swiftly to the characteristic slightly pointed top. Perhaps this modified hemisphere is a form that emerges naturally when building simply with pieces of stone, since we find similar structural forms again in the Nuraghi of Sardinia and, even today, in the exclusive vernacular of the Trulli in Apulia.

Of course the domed interior recalls the cave, but a dry, neat, definable cave, cosy in the case of the domestic huts, which are small. The tombs of Mycenae approach very close to the cave, and what we have called excavation architecture, since the shaping of the tomb involved what was actually a cutting away process, and the tombs themselves are covered, and were perhaps totally concealed by turf. It seems logical, though, to group them with the domes, many of which do in fact surmount an 'excavated' type of building.

It does not matter for our purpose of trying to define and account for the character of a building whether the dome shape emerges from corbelling or from a system of voussoirs, or even, for that matter, from setting ribs as a framework for concrete or rubble. The dome in formal building, if we exclude the Mycenaean example, undoubtedly first appears under Rome, where the grandest is the Pantheon.

The emotional impact felt by so many people upon entering the Pantheon, p30, p131 29 compacted of a curious combination of awe and elation, is difficult to account for, but I think would be attributed by most observers to the simplicity of its shape and the magnificence of its scale. There may be, as has been suggested, an unconscious satisfaction at its mathematical relations, which are such that the dome could be inverted exactly in the available height below its springing to form a complete sphere: internally, necessarily, for a dome is seldom reflected on its outer surfaces as an exact counterpart of its interior form, and thus partakes, to some extent, of the character of 'excavated' architecture. The Pantheon could appear as more of a cavity than it does, were it not for its culminating eye, which shows the relatively wafer thin section through the top of the dome and seems to pierce and admit the ether. The resulting graded lighting that passes over the coffers of the dome and merges with the shadows of the niches in the lower wall seems to define the gradual thickening of the wall, so that although we can see the sharp glinting edge of the circumference of the oculus we are also strongly aware of an almost impenetrable thickness of wall at the base where we stand, a thickness that as we have shown* is at least partly indicated by the quite deep recesses that are gouged into it. The surface

* On p. 28 above.

27   28

of the walls is given some assessable scale by the classical method of subdivision by orders and entablatures, and the vast disc of the floor must always have been measured by a regular pattern moving in multiple perspective in all directions towards the periphery. A circular plan has no axis, unless one imagines a vertical one at its centre, and when it is bounded by a cylindrical wall it projects a sense of total enclosure, which is enormously emphasized by a dome, so that all surfaces except the floor fuse into each other and become one powerful containing control. I have called this 'cosy' in the case of the small hut, and on that scale it can be as comfortable as a tea cosy, but in the vast space of the Pantheon the enclosure is remote from imagined contact, rendered somehow even remoter by the opening so far above. The human visitor stands below in an isolation almost as profound as he experiences in communication with the celestial dome itself.

29, p131 The great cage of the portico erected against the cylinder has been criticized as a clumsy adjunct. The compromise arises from the fact that any entrance into a circular plan is basically arbitrary. A *deus ex machina* through the oculus would be the only propriety. As it is the architect has probably done what he could. At least the scale of the portico columns cannot be criticized. The rotunda is almost overwhelmingly complete. In one structure this great Roman architect made the ultimate statement of a dome on continuous support. It was echoed and repeated everywhere, like the eddies of a pond. But it was never exceeded, nor even equalled in size or implication. The only thing waiting to be done with it was to lift it on to a more sophisticated base.

p30 It is the continuity of the dome downwards that gives the sense of enclosure in the Pantheon. Most later domes are supported on pendentives, and present an effect of suspension which is quite different. The dome of Santa Sophia at Istanbul has often been compared to a bubble, and certainly the fact that most 28, p132 domes of any size are so high above the floor leads them to an ambiguity of size and weight. The dome of Santa Sophia has no drum, and it is pierced around

29   30

the base with windows. This reduces the hemisphere and at the same time evidences the fact that, as with other Byzantine domes, the inside and outside are faces of the same material structure. The lightness of the dome is further emphasized by its booster of half-domes, and the continuance of windows pierced high in the clerestory walls.*

For a follow-up in the West to this confidence in the building of domed structures we have to leap across virtually the whole of the Middle Ages to fifteenth-century Florence, where, nearly one thousand years after Santa Sophia, Brunelleschi raised his great dome over the brittle base of Florence 32 Cathedral. This, the first dome of the Renaissance world, is in fact beehive-shaped, rising to a slight point on which the lantern is supported. This is explained by the fact that Brunelleschi was drawing on a medieval way of constructing with a ribbed framework,† which had been developed along with the pointed arch and vault and their more vertical thrust. It was impossible to devise centering of the kind normally used in vaults for a dome of these dimensions, set as it was so high above the floor of the church, and it was necessary to design a structure that would support itself as work proceeded. Brunelleschi's solution, as we have seen, was the use of a curve more vertical than a hemisphere, with two thicknesses of masonry tied together at intervals and forming props to each other. Between these two skins of the dome winds a stair that leads to the lantern and is supported against the controlled swelling of the inner layer. Internally the dome rests easily on its great piers, creating a vast centralizing crossing to the unpretentious but gaunt nave. Externally a system of half domes lifts the great central dome on its polygonal drum like a big ship riding calmly on the rough seas of Florentine roofs, transmuting what is otherwise a large but indifferent box into one of the great cathedrals of the world.

In the enormous number of domed churches that rose after the middle of the fifteenth century there is usually more integration between the structure of the crossing and that of the rest of the church than we find in Santa Maria del Fiore. Brunelleschi himself perhaps never quite achieved this integration, except in the Pazzi Chapel. In his larger churches he was too concerned with 30 making the eastern complex into a centralized statement, and this in itself prevents its fusion with the nave. In the Pazzi Chapel there is no nave, and the interior is a very fastidious follow-up to the cupola and vault of the portico, but the character of this whole chapel is that of a delicate box-cage complex. Perhaps the centralized church of Santa Maria degli Angeli (never completed to his design) would have presented the most enclosed of all Brunelleschi's spaces, though not precisely of a beehive type.

The dome takes on a beehive character of enclosure only when it is extended

* See also discussion on p. 98.   † See also p. 40 above.

by a drum. When this occurs over a crossing, unless it is extremely wide, the dome often creates a spatial zone of its own, separated from the lower spaces of nave, aisles, and transepts, which merge with each other below it. This may be one of the reasons why later churches suppress the aisles, either by excluding them altogether, or making them very narrow, or curtailing their function as p135 ambulatories by replacing them with a series of almost separated bays or chapels. The dome then bestrides the full width of the nave which it follows with more spatial logic. The difficulty of attaching or welding a fully expressed dome to almost any kind of nave clearly embarrassed architects of this time, who usually seem to have pressed for a centralized plan when possible.* In these, especially where the plan is circular or polygonal, rather than cruciform, we find the full character of the dome expressed, either very simply, as in countless baptistries all over Italy dating from the earliest period of church building, or in churches like San Vitale in Ravenna, or, ultimately, with the full Baroque as shown in Santa Maria della Salute in Venice.

Only in such buildings does the dome reach its full statement. Where it is most successfully used as roofing on other than round or polygonal areas, it is multiplied, and so loses its 'beehive' character. In churches with Byzantine 57 antecedents, like St. Mark's at Venice, or the churches of south-western France, naves and transepts are roofed by a series of cupolas, which express themselves more as canopies, and belong in a different section of our analysis.

If man devised the hive, the bee is wholly responsible for the honeycomb, and although human beings have not on the whole been able to borrow directly the structural perfection of the hexagon for habitation purposes, they have been quick to learn the lesson of the economy of the multiple. From tenement to

* For instance the successive architects of St. Peter's at Rome, and later Wren at St. Paul's in London.

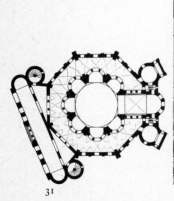

31   32   33

luxury apartment, from Roman insula to modern skyscraper, the repetition in a block of space-units has made possible the kind of centralization necessary in a large town.

Where the hive, large or small, is essentially one closely defined internal space, the honeycomb is a regularly compartmented block, whose character is an external one. Ideally the compartments are identical, and theoretically they are repeatable infinitely. The more closely the block approaches these two requirements, the more perfectly does it emulate the character of the honeycomb, which like itself is limited only by practical considerations.

Practical and, one may tentatively say, aesthetic, in the case of man's contribution. For though immeasurably large effects have been long since categorized as sublime, sublimity of this sort can cripple the city image. But perhaps the main limitation is practical after all, as any definable entity is in itself one thing and has to be managed or controlled as one thing. Still the repeatability of the unit is the significant quality of the honeycomb, and therefore, one supposes, should determine the architectural character of the multiple unit building, whether intended for residential or other purposes. Here the International Style has made a contribution by defining several principles incontrovertibly valid:

(*a*) If there is one aspect agreed to be the best for any unit, then all units in the block serving the same purpose should ideally have that aspect.
(*b*) The same applies to admission of light and air and internal planning and subdivision.
(*c*) If several units are serving the same purpose they should look as if they are.
(*d*) Architecturally a block of units is a whole and should appear as such.

Points *c* and *d* possibly contributed in causing the word 'functional' to be used of buildings of this class, though, as can be clearly seen, they are aesthetic considerations. However all aesthetic control implies some sort of order, and all order leads to some extent to smoother functioning, so perhaps there is some justification for the use of the term. In any case 'functional' is an aesthetic term when used of a building.* What is meant is that it looks as if it works, whether or not it actually does. With regard to *d* above, a block containing one sort of unit may be expressed differently from a block of another sort, and of course is logically differentiated from the storey or area below or in some cases above it. This may be done by means of Le Corbusier's *pilotis*, but there is a variety of possible treatments.

It is no coincidence that the honeycomb, being the natural fabrication of

* See also above p. 10.

living creatures, should be an example of structural precision and economy. If
we wish to see it exemplified by human ingenuity therefore, we shall not be
surprised to find its principles understood and emulated by the Romans in
structures like amphitheatres where height is acquired by a neat fitting together
of repeating units. It is true that the Romans did not go so far as to achieve
their multi-storeyed elevations by fitting units, like those of the honeycomb itself,
into each other to form the reticular pattern with which we are familiar, though
the principle of the reticule was understood and used by them as a brick face.
The repeated vaulted units are set side by side and given a horizontal base
resting on top of the row of vaulted units below. But once the strength
developed by the masonry vault is understood, it forms a reasonably economical
method of building and can be used (if we consider the Colosseum in Rome) on
a very considerable scale. Something even of the cohesion of the honeycomb is
achieved, not only actually by the use of mortar, but visually by the continuous
relationship of the structural units made possible by the curve of the elliptical
building. The Romans used this system of supporting vaults in other multi-
storeyed buildings, for example at Trajan's Forum where layers of shops were
built upon each other, and here, as with the various kinds of auditoria and
'grandstands', the construction was a honeycomb in depth as well as height.

The alternation of the honeycomb units to form the characteristic diagonal
relationship has not to any great extent been emulated by the human builder.
Safdie has used polygonal sections for the units of one of his housing blocks,
and Goodovitch has also designed a block with this kind of unit.* On the whole

* Moshe Safdie is the architect of Habitat, a residential complex that made a great impression at
Expo 67 held in Montreal; see pp. 85–6 below. Goodovitch is another Israeli architect.

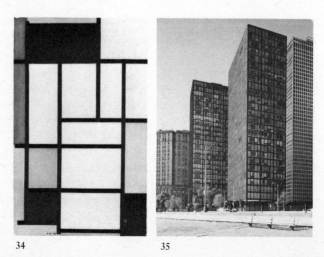

34   35

though the weight and need for a compressive resolution seem to have contributed to the continued reliance on vertical and horizontal support. It is perhaps the 'eggbox' compromise that comes nearest to a honeycomb section in contemporary building. Orderly vertical extension of the structural unit has followed the multi-windowed building in its development through the twentieth century, but the perfect eggbox is displayed in those elegant shallow blocks which architects like Le Corbusier raised on *pilotis* in the first half of the century, 70, p147 the constructional and space units perfectly repeated and therefore all with the same aspect.

The Cell and the Cluster

Both of these types are meant to suggest a non-geometric type of design, and also a growth-relationship that may allow the one to develop (ideologically if not literally) into the other. One does not want to force the analogy just because it has some imaginative or verbal appeal, but I had in mind, when groping for a classification which ultimately produced the word 'cell', Le Corbusier's chapel at 36, 37 Ronchamp, which did not seem to fit into any other classification. If a cell is the simplest possible unit of life, then Ronchamp cannot be said to be a cell, for it is complex and sophisticated; but if we can regard some cells as being those two things in potential, an embryo (if we may mix our analogies) of whatever elaboration may be expected of their kind, then perhaps we can see Ronchamp as this: a single space, after all, which is vitalist rather than geometric, or as we used to say, 'biomorphic'.

The chapel at Ronchamp is difficult to analyse descriptively, but it has an impact on the visitor that is simplified by its evident consistency. First of all, to say it is freely shaped is not to say it is amorphous, though this is a word some architects are now curiously prepared to use about their designing. The shapes indicated on plan are in fact powerful and purposive. Each length of wall defines part of the total enclosure, while curling around minor zones (chapels) separating them partly from the major internal space, yet by their unhesitating continuity keeping them a part of it; there are no rectangularities or 'corners'. The south wall is particularly powerful, a 'membrane' Le Corbusier has called it, which increases in thickness from west to east and from ground to roof. This thickness is not lost between the two surfaces of the wall, but is revealed again and again by the scattered light-holes over its vertical area. Each section of wall is freely articulated from the next, and the flexibility of the links is ensured by making them great doorways, in scale with the building as a whole and not gauged to minimal physical needs. The doors themselves are of unusually heavy material (stone or metal) and thus defy any appearance of being crushed between the massive walls. Le Corbusier did not approve of stained glass in modern architecture, so the glass of the light-openings is coloured and defined as a plane by drawings and word-images like 'Marie'.

The freedom of the plan and absence of any regularly placed supports indicates that the roof must be a separate element containing its own means to rigidity, lying across the curling walls. In fact the roof is the most spectacular element of the building. It is separated by a streak of light from the tops of the walls, to emphasize its separateness, and is formed by two 'membranes' providing insulation between them. These are not continuously horizontal but curve up to form the now famous 'coif' effect, which throws water back upon itself towards a simple drainage system through gargoyles from the lowest part of the roof into the decorative rain-water tank. This quite small building is very great architecture.

One of the powerful emotional evocations of the Ronchamp chapel is to promote (and the response seems intestinal rather than cerebral) the reaching back to something primeval and elemental. The nature of a cell is to form part of a group or 'cluster', and perhaps the isolated cell is rare in building tradition. Even where it is not in contact with other cells it will usually be found in their 27 company. African kraals give an obvious example of this, and usually we shall find the genre in vernacular building rather than formal and therefore more sophisticated architecture.

In despite of this a 'cell' type of construction has recently been experimented with, that is to say a type of single-space independent structure: a phere, a half sphere, in plastic or glass, a shell, expanded or framed (geodesic)[5] and propounding the problem, of course, of how to subdivide or arrange within for living. A single person often lives with no frustration in a single cell, if it is zoned for his necessary activities and can contain him and his paraphernalia.

36

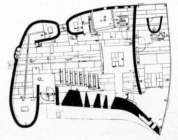

37

Two human beings present more than twice the problem. Two fused bubbles
are not necessarily the answer to activities that must be part shared and part
private. The curved surface, which may be a bubble or geometrically spher-
oidal, has become popularly 'organic', which among other ideas can include that
of growth or expansion by not having a tightly defined external limit. Even early
and Renaissance classical architects liked the idea of the shapes and relations of
the parts of a building relating to those of the human body. Supporters of
organic theories of architecture, including in latter times Frank Lloyd Wright,
were concerned about total integration, for example between house and setting.
In 1910 he defined an organic system as 'one great thing instead of a quarrelling
collection of little things'.[6] Bruno Zevi considers that Frank Lloyd Wright
interprets the open plan 'organically and with a full sense of humanity'.[7]
Perhaps more recently still organic architecture has been identified with 'free-
form' and therefore non-rectangular or rectilinear designing. Hundertwasser's
1958 'Manifesto' considered, or affected to consider, the ruler—i.e. the straight-
edge—as 'the symptom of the new sickness of decadence', but perhaps we
prefer the definition of 'organics' of William Kataroles, who (in 1960)
propounded that houses 'would grow to certain sizes, subdivide or fuse for
larger functions'.[8] In the context of the cell this is confined to containers,
however irregular, whether curved or angled, returning upon themselves and
involving problems of mini-zoning rather than subdivision.

    If cells combine, as even bubbles may, they form a cluster. This too, in
building, tends to be a vernacular development, simply a series of cells, huddled
together like barnacles for mutual support, social and physical. This is the
character of many troglodytic groups, half excavated (or using existing caves)
and half constructed as they usually are. It also becomes the character of groups
of dwellings which support themselves, or partly support themselves, upon each
other. There is a wide geographical spread of this kind of building, which is
often of a soft construction, like mud or unbaked brick, with not much strength
in itself. The Pueblo and adobe villages in parts of America are examples, still
to be found for instance in New Mexico and Colorado.[9] Arab villages in North
Africa sometimes have this character, so do the clusters of building on islands
like Samos. Clusters of cells which do not necessarily make use of each other's
walls, preserving a total roundness, are common in African kraals and other
areas using a traditional vernacular like the Trulli of south-eastern Italy.

    The use of a cluster is more of a potential than an actuality in formal
architecture, although one could argue that any grouping of rooms is a sophisticated development of the grouping of cells. There is a difference however:
rooms in the usual sense result from the subdivision of a space, while the
'cluster' of 'cells' as here defined is an agglomeration (but not simply a 'piling

or 'massing' as so many so-called multi-cellular buildings are today). Perhaps
the nearest thing to this in historic western architecture was the Cretan palace
38 of Minoan times. The plans of Knossos, Phaestos, and Mallia are difficult to
read, especially as the buildings are, except where there have been reconstruc-
tions, little more than foundations with a few feet of rubble wall standing; until
one begins to see what they have in common. First of all there is the large
central court, now believed to have been associated with ritual bull-games,
which have been reconstructed in various ways. On to this court open some of
the larger and more important rooms, which have in their turn small courts and
wells for light and ventilation. The outer walls do not form the continuous
façades to which we are accustomed in other great buildings of the time or later
(for instance in Egypt) and this with the fragmentary remains of superimposed
building can produce a somewhat perplexing result, until one realizes (as J. W.
Graham has so clearly demonstrated[10]) that the palace has been designed and
built from the court outwards, each room added to the previous one in the
manner and size needed, without reference to an exterior boundary, which may
not ever finally be reached.

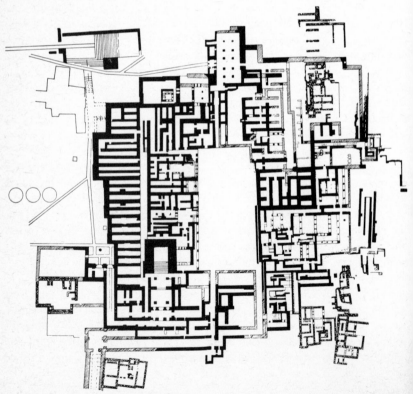

The megaron system of arrangement makes this possible, as considerable apartments (and many quite small chambers) lead between pillars, to which are attached the leaves of widely opening doors, on to a covered loggia, and then a light well, preserving privacy while admitting light and air. Provided these wells are preserved and respected several storeys can be built, and rooms almost indefinitely added next to, or partly over, those existing. In reading the floor plan, therefore, one needs an alertness in recording where the levels change. This changing and stepping of levels is complicated by the fact that the ancient Cretans worshipped the Cthonic or Earth gods, and therefore the palaces have a number of pits and lustral chambers descending to the lowest convenient level to bring them into contact with the earth. Clustering takes place on the vertical as well as the horizontal as there are no continuous floor levels throughout the building.

Zoning shows a surprising consistency from one palace to another. In general main reception and formal halls seem to lie west of the great court, kitchens and food stores and possibly dining areas to the north, and women's and domestic quarters and galleries, for viewing whatever activities took place in the court, to the east. The zone south of the court in all these palaces is the most lightly and thinly planned, and may have formed a convenient approach direction. On this system of plan development the peripheral walls have no special architectural meaning as they do not appear ever to represent a final structure. Of course they were tidily finished off, the same fine craftsmanship and sense of decoration being applied to the recesses and breaks in the walls, and with the colour and resulting zones of sharp light and shadow it must have presented a glinting and assertive bulk.

With their character of modulated surface and possible accretion these palaces seem truly 'clusters', and it is surely not without relevance that they have been likened to towns (complex and self-sufficient social organisms) or that what we know of the Cretan town proper, like Gournia, shows a development not dissimilar to that of the palace, with the public square as the great court, and the building of the chief or prince taking the place of throne rooms and reception halls. In all cases the thinking, as well as the actual development, is from the centre outwards, and it may thus be considered an embryo of that kind of expanding settled community cluster which is not limited and defined by encircling defensive walls. In its simplest form it could be adequate only for the type of community which is linked by tribal affinity, service to a ruler, or that kind of poverty which imposes on the simple inhabitants absolute dependence on each other.

An imaginative and exciting version of the cluster appeared at Montreal 39 during Expo 67 with Moshe Safdie's Habitat. The principle here is what the architect calls terraced housing mounted on A-frames 'under which are the public facilities, shops, the art gallery, the school, and offices'. The complex has to be seen from the air or in the form of a model to read a general impression, while probably sectional drawings will here be more meaningful than plans. Each 'cell' or basic space-shape is called by the architect a box or module, and in discussing a later project he talks of the groups of modules as 'clusters'. One residence may involve several modules: that is to say, perhaps, several 'cells', like a bunch of grapes rather than the segments of an orange.[11]

Visually and intellectually this is a break-away from the eggbox or even honeycomb, though the latter is also an assemblage rather than a subdivision. The assemblage is clearly more flexible, since, not having a structurally determined periphery it is not limited in space—or time.

39

Scaffold and Skeleton

The Gothic cathedral is sometimes described as a building wearing its skeleton on the outside, and although this is not an exact analogy of the function of buttresses, it is true that all framed structures provide a system of support not unlike that of the bone structure of vertebrates. This applies to the half-timbered or any other 'frame' house, and to many reinforced concrete and steel buildings of our own century as much as to the thirteenth-century cathedral, but it is more spectacularly evident in the latter, and has therefore caught the imagination more. Perhaps also it seems more marvellous that a medium with the gravity of stone, which has in itself so little tensile strength or elasticity, should have been used to develop such a resilient effect. The quadrant arches under the tribune roof of a Romanesque church seem not at all to presage in effect the permissive flying buttress, although it is really only the removal of the roof and outer wall of the tribune that leads to the startlingly different looking supporting system.

When all is said and done what one can read externally is the old basilican shape of narrower nave rising higher than side aisles to form a clerestory, and that the nave walls have risen so high that they have come to need an elaborate prop. What can also be read is that these props occur between the clerestory windows, making them possible, and that therefore the roof is supported on a system of piers, so that the wall between (in this case almost entirely glass) is non-supporting. It has been observed that in High Gothic the mouldings of windows, being now bar-tracery and not the surface-preserving plate tracery of Romanesque, lead the eye and thinking outward to relate interior and exterior space, but this is really hindered by the plane of the glass, when coloured as it ideally was. From outside it is a dark, wholly definitive surface, and from inside, 24 translucent as its necessary character is, it is nevertheless as much of a defining plane as though it were opaque. It has not even a partial transparency, and although it might (as Frankl says[12]) define the centre of the wall thickness, it is only knowledge of the exterior that interprets the tracery as leading outwards. It could in fact be argued that the interior of a Gothic church is more enclosed than the Romanesque, for the latter, by the very piercing of its dark wall surfaces, refers all the time to the light and space outside. The Gothic never invites the imagination to stray beyond its own self-sufficient organization of interior space.

If the side walls of the Gothic cathedral are not fully explicit structurally, the west end is even less so. Again it has been suggested that ideally some reflection of the interior system should show here, and perhaps architecturally speaking this claim could be justified, as it could in the case of façades of 'buried' Baroque buildings, but in fact it has seldom been achieved, and except for the desire for continuity and the expectancy arising in any well designed entrance zone, it is not easy to see whether architects expended much energy on this. The plan at once shows why. The west end traditionally incorporates the p134 towers, which must express themselves as well as contribute to a unity of the west façade. The portals do not necessarily enter directly into nave and aisles,* and there is no reason therefore why they should be designed as though they do. The gable, which, again traditionally, reveals itself behind the lacework of the web that links the towers, is indicative of the setting back of the nave itself behind the towers. Only within the nave is the vaulting system fully demonstrated. Here we see, if we have remembered, why the high walls need the series

---

* There is usually a pause before one steps out into the westernmost bays where the regular vaulting system starts.

of props outside; although it has been contended that the buttresses are un-
necessary, and that because masonry laid in mortar tends to become more and
more of a monolithic structure, undue thrusts from the vaults lessen as time
goes on, producing an almost entirely compressive load. The props are there
perhaps because they seemed necessary, and by the same token look reassuring.
It may emerge that medieval buttresses are pure scaffolding: self-supporting
members that do not involve themselves with the stress movements of the
actual building. Scaffolding however does sometimes use the structures which it
serves to hold itself rigid, and masonry (and other) props may well be found to
be in equivocal relationship with the building in question.

More clearly to be analysed are buildings which have dispensed, or almost so,
with infilling of the structural frame. Most bridges and gantries fall into this
41 class, and of course isolated monuments such as the Eiffel Tower. The Eiffel
Tower is perhaps not a monument proper, in that it does not commemorate
anything, except of course the 1889 Exhibition, and, in the event, its designer,
but it partakes to some extent of the crystal, if that is not too far-fetched, a
crystal of space. It also obviously falls into the tower or post category, in that its
purpose was solely to achieve height, from which to be able to see as far as
possible. But its skeletal quality can hardly be ignored, and it brings architecture to the brink of engineering, a situation which has been discussed earlier.

Structures with a strong motivation of function which are left as almost pure
scaffolding or triangulated frame structure are not normally claimed to have
high architectural quality. In this class would be contained such things as
windmills, water towers, radio towers, radar structures, beacons, pylons carrying high voltage electrical cables. Few of these have the individual structural

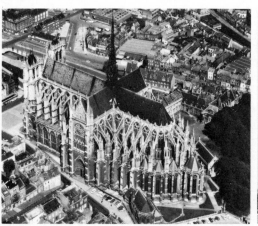 

40   41

audacity or character that singles out an event like the building of the Eiffel Tower for special wonder, but often they make a positive enough assertion to render them acceptable in the environment and thus may be said to bring engineering to the brink of architecture. A series of cable pylons in particular often achieves a delicate grace in crossing the lands carrying their loops of wire. More specifically of architectural intention have been bell-towers of churches, sometimes of wood open-frame construction, sometimes of reinforced concrete or steel. A distinguished example of the latter is Frei Otto's bell-tower of the Evangelist Church in Berlin-Shönow of 1963, in which he collaborated with the architect Ewald Bubner.[13] This was a pre-fabricated steel construction erected in one operation including the hanging of the three bells. The height is 78 feet. A cat ladder clings to one of the four vertical corners. The design is a pure single grid with rounded corners and no joints visible. Angle-iron provides the required rigidity, as of course does the grid treatment itself, allowing passage of the wind. Is it seemly, one wonders, for the ancient mechanism of a bell with clappers to depend from this efficiently modern tower? One might almost postulate a siren. But of course all the functions of a church are ancient.

A more complex structure was projected by Louis Kahn in the late 1950s as a 'city tower', basically helical and hexagonal, to be framed up tetrahedrons and octohedrons. It was designed for a possible 660 feet.[14] 'Space frames' have intrigued many architects in fact over a couple of decades. Buckminster Fuller is one of the best-known with his *Tensegrity* structure, *Climatron*, and other spherical buildings based on triangulation.[15] The great framed 'tower' of the John Hancock building in Chicago designed by Graham of the firm of Skidmore Owings and Merrill, has giant diagonals to aid the vertical and horizontal framework to rigidity.[16]

Space forms of a purer type have come from the hands of technically orientated architects like the German Konrad Wachsman who concentrated on the development of 'structural units', particularly in timber. With his various units he devised systems for the construction of vast halls and hangars. If we go back to structural developments early in the century we find a 'skeleton' type in relatively widespread use. One was Max Berg's vast braced dome of 1912–13 in the Centenary Hall in Breslau; Perret's gaunt concrete church at Le Raincy (1922–3); and Karl Moser's equally rawboned St. Anthony at Basle (1926–7).[17] We must not forget, either, the skeletal spires of Gaudi's Sagrada Famiglia in Barcelona, on which he worked from 1883 until his death in 1926, and which he never completed.

The contemporary space frame traces its origin to the middle of the nineteenth century when such buildings as the Crystal Palace and other conservatories of glass and iron were first erected. The covering of railway stations and other areas involving wide span had by the end of the century developed an extensive vocabulary in which were produced a range of significant buildings. The great exhibitions that followed the British lead of 1851 provided some of the best opportunities for this kind of experiment, since what was wanted in the first place was a large containing area, probably temporary and therefore not of 'aesthetic' concern either (one presumes) to promoters or public. One of the buildings to emerge from this kind of situation was the Machine Hall of the International Exhibition of 1889 in Paris, by Dutert and Contamin, with three-hinge frames carrying the great glass top. The techniques gradually found their way into buildings destined for less ephemeral use, for instance the three libraries designed for Paris, the Sainte Geneviève (1843), the Impériale (1855), and the Nationale (1858–68), all by Henri Labrouste, who was one of the earliest to be involved with this kind of construction, but followed by many in the latter half of the century.

It was only a step, but a significant one, to the use of framed construction in general. At first it tended to be concealed by a traditional 'face', and as such does not fall properly into our class of 'skeleton' building. A factory near Paris designed by Jules Saulnier (1871–2) is an early display of visible frame con-struction.[18] In America Le Baron Jenney in his Home Insurance Building of 1883 showed his framework construction, and the Chicago School in general evolved the frame into the well-known grid with non-supporting infilling that became common vocabulary for the high-rise building, until the structure once again retired behind glass and sheet metal cladding and the curtain wall. It is difficult to find in the early years of frame construction buildings that excite anything beyond an approval of slowly maturing awareness. There are a few piquant exceptions, like the Perret flats in the Rue Franklin of 1902, which Le
42 Corbusier called 'a manifesto'![19] There is also the Peter Behrens factory of

42   43

1910–1.[20] But Gropius had already used a curtain wall at Dessau, Mies had projected his glass skyscraper (1921),[21] and Le Corbusier though he had at once realized the potential of the skyscraper, had designed his own city in 1922 with an internal construction system. The 'skeleton' reappears from time to time. A late design of Fero Saarinen (who died in 1961) was the Dulles Airport which shows a substantial set of concrete 'ribs' supporting an inverted curve of roof, the infilling being glazing. In general in the 1960s the skeleton seems to have been less popular than the scaffold as an external effect, with the frame supporting little beside itself, and perhaps the roof. Sometimes this has arisen out of a desire for a protective screen, as with Le Corbusier at Chandigarh.[22] Of course 43 Chandigarh involves something more complicated than this. Le Corbusier's material has always been concrete and its massy surfaces must not be allowed to distract observance of its often skeletal function. The Chandigarh Assembly is virtually hypostyle with a canopy over the pierced blade-bones of the entrance.

Bridges and Barricades

Bridges, particularly modern bridges, are not normally regarded as architecture, but are considered to belong properly to the province of the engineer. It is true they are not, in the sense we have defined, containers; nor do they usually afford any sort of overhead protection; yet they relate to human occupation in a similar way to other structures that we have considered here, and are especially interesting as a group that has passed in the course of time from the hands of the architect to those of the engineer.[23]

The idea of bridging is in itself such a basic one that it has not been convenient to characterize it, as we have all the other types considered, through some familiar shape or object, though it is traditional for engineers themselves to regard bridges as falling into three classes which are explained in terms of primitive usage: a bridge is a way of spanning a gap, whatever the nature of that gap. Usually we think of rivers or canals, but it may be a ravine or cleft in the earth, or merely uneven terrain, or in modern times a road or a railway. The simplest type of bridge may be likened to a fallen tree stretched across the gap to be spanned; the second type would be like stepping stones across a river bed, or street (as in old towns where the street carried refuse or rainwater); the third type has been compared to the use of the hanging or projecting branches of trees or creepers on opposite sides of the gap, which could be joined, or which could provide a means of swinging oneself across to the other side.[24]

Ancient bridges were usually the result of combining the first two types mentioned: that is the 'tree trunk' stretched across a series of 'stepping stones', one section at a time, or in building terms a horizontal surface resting on a row of piers. The Romans, who were very successful bridge builders, used arches to span the river, as large as possible to keep down the number of piers to be sunk in the river bed and therefore to impede as little as possible the flow of the water. In Rome itself the Mulvian Bridge still stands across the Tiber, its semi-circular arches springing from the plinths of heavy piers, and bridges of this kind were built throughout the Roman Empire. Particularly distinguished bridges are some which were used as aqueducts. One of the oldest is the Aqua Claudia, a single arcade carrying water across the Roman Campagna, but more exciting is the famous Pont du Gard, near Nîmes, where three ranges of arches in rugged stone form one of the most distinguished structures left by antiquity. With their breakwater (or cutwater) edges presented to the flow of the river and their sturdy arches surmounted by a roadway, this was so excellent a way of spanning a river that it remained the standard way of building bridges right into the nineteenth century.

With a certain margin for variation possible in the proportioning of arches and piers, and the finishing and decoration of surfaces and balustrades, the bridge was an extension of the architect's responsibilities and in fact so attractive were its implications that it appeared in smaller, more ornamental versions, sometimes miniature, in the parks and gardens of wealthy patrons, particularly of the eighteenth century. 'Palladian' bridges were designed by almost all of the architects of any note, usually (for the streams they spanned tended to be narrow) of single span, the proportions and ornament carefully ordered.

The bridge passed into the hands of the engineer when the old Roman method began to be superseded by the extended possibilities of iron, steel, and concrete, although it was some time before the full value of mathematical calculation was appreciated. The first attempt at a cast-iron bridge was made at
44 Lyons as early as 1755, and by 1779 the Coalbrookdale Bridge had been con-

44   45

structed by Abraham Darby and John Wilkinson, with a single arch spanning the river, supported by masonry on the banks. Stone bridges continued to be built, and with these architects were still associated: Robert Mylne designed the Blackfriars Bridge with elliptical arches. Metal however was the material of the engineer. Southwark, by the famous John Rennie, was a cast iron bridge, completed in 1819, while in the same year Telford, who had designed the iron bridge over the Severn at Buildwas nearly twenty-five years earlier, began the great suspension bridge over the Menai Straits. With the development of the suspension bridge the distances spanned could be considerably increased. The Menai Bridge had a clear span of 550 feet hung from two main piers.

Other suspension bridges followed: at Bristol, by Brunel, 700 feet, and by the same great engineer, Hungerford, 676 feet central span, and trussed bridges like his Royal Albert at Saltash which had two river spans of 455 feet each and a total length of 2,200 feet. 45

The use of steel increased the possibilities of the suspension bridge, which, hung on enormous cables from pier towers as near as possible to the banks, provided the longest and most impressive spans over water. With the development in France in the first half of the nineteenth century of reinforced concrete with its combined tensile and compressive strength, the possibilities of advance in constructive design increased to provide the breathtaking bridging feats we know today. Some of the most visually arresting bridges are those which span ravines and valleys in high mountains. For these reinforced concrete is normally used, and the constructional method often resembles the position of a climber in a rock 'chimney', limbs exerted outwards to maintain the stretch. 46

A bridge is a means by which a roadway may be continued and in modern times becomes a part of motorway construction, sometimes in fact forming the motorway itself. An early adaptation of this sort was the bridging of railway lines for the safe passage of vehicular traffic; the bearing of the actual railway over rivers and ravines had long been a part of the duties of the viaduct. A

46 47

special type of bridge emerging directly from the railway system is the bridge
for foot passengers, essentially a link between platforms and frequently covered
and even enclosed. This did not normally present spanning problems and could
easily be provided as a frame construction approached by stairways or lifts. The
footbridge over the busy traffic-way was a logical development: these were often
framed metal in the early days, reinforced concrete later. They came eventually
to carry vehicular traffic and are today a normal way for subsidiary roads to
cross motorways. An important development before the war was the 'clover
leaf' or similar approach to the motorway itself by means of which large sections of the road were raised above the surrounding ground levels and carried
on stanchions or other supports.

The bridge as an accommodation building is probably rare, though the
problem of linking the parts of a building complex will no doubt continue to be
solved by various types of bridges. The Bridge of Sighs at Venice which
formed part of a corridor between the Ducal Palace and its prisons, crossing a
canal, is an old and familiar example, but there are many such. Perhaps the
Rialto Bridge, also in Venice, could be regarded at least partly as 'accommodational', for it was designed to carry shops over the Grand Canal, and thus
link two shopping areas, the Merceria and the market. The Ponte Vecchio in
Florence performs a similar function, the untidy projections of the backs of
jewellers' booths on both sides of the bridge, acceptable only to the romantic-
minded but familiar to the tourist. More significant as architecture must have
been the Bon Marché department store in Paris built by Eiffel and Boileau in
1876, which displayed 'an airy system of footbridges, supported by slender
columns and lit by the large glazed roof'.[25] Architects have occasionally used a
bridge theme for houses, and one may be mentioned here: a house projected by
the American architect Craig Ellwood to span a gorge in California. But any
house carried above ground on *pilotis* or other supports is using the bridge
principle to some extent. Kenzo Tange's project for the reorganization of the
Tsukiji district of Tokyo in 1960 involves multi-storeyed office buildings with a
system of bridges connecting vertical blocks. This enormously increases available movement-areas at the lowest levels and proposes upper floor circulation of
an unprecedented kind.

A bridge links, a barricade separates, though in fact it may provide a level
platform for circulation. The whole problem of bridge construction is that of
spanning without impeding the flow of water or traffic of any sort beneath and
past it. A barricade is specifically designed to bar the flow, and any foot or
trafficway it supports is not a bridge in the true sense, since it does not span.
The kind of barricade which superficially most closely resembles a bridge is a
lock or dam, both of which permit the flow of water from time to time. Though

again engineers and not architects are appointed to design dams, this is the kind
of structure which in a simpler form was entrusted to architects, and which
today carries often a powerful aesthetic.

If we turn to buildings that could be regarded as barricades, then the further
back we go in history, the more closely they were identified with the responsibilities of architects. City walls, with or without bastions, and actual fortifications, were entrusted to architects from antiquity to the eighteenth century.
One of the most eminent of Italian architects, Michele Sanmicheli, is associated
with more military than civil works (halfway between them perhaps are his
handsome gates at Verona); Leonardo was the Sforza family defence engineer;
Michelangelo was involved with Papal walls and forts. Perhaps the medieval
castle is the most obvious type of building to qualify for the 'barricade' classification. If we take as an example Harlech Castle we have a pattern especially
designed to prevent access. Characteristic are the moat (with easily manipulated
drawbridge), thick walls with crenellated walkways at the top of them and
defensive towers at the salient angles, and the keep, the last bastion, part tower
and part refuge, to which were attached further defensive angle turrets, and
which contained what domestic quarters there were. This 'defensive' mode of
building lingered on in English manor house design, part tradition, part caution, and part a conscious nostalgia. These houses however do not really fall
into our 'barricade' group, which rather consists of buildings with this appear- p137
ance conditioned by other necessities, often visual.

If a barricade holds forces out, as with a fortress, it also holds forces in, as
with a prison: dungeons are often caves, and prisons cages, but a third type falls
rather into the barricade class, a building meant for self-immolation, and indeed
keeps the world out as much as it keeps its inmates within its walls, that is the
convent or monastery, of which a magnificent example is Le Corbusier's La 47
Tourette near Lyons. The sheer rugged walls, as much as the monitory notices
planted about the terrain, remind us that here the profane is excluded and the
contemplative protected. Albi Cathedral takes the form of a barricade, perhaps
for a purpose similar to that of the convent, to imply the spiritual seclusion and
the rejection of the world,* and so does the Vatican precinct, round whose
menacing walls the pilgrim and tourist have exhaustingly to trudge before
entrance can be effected.

All walls that serve the purpose of exclusion or seclusion are barricades, even
if the field of operation is purely visual. Garden walls, screen walls, walls that
act as partitions in a system of otherwise open planning are all, architecturally,
barricades.

---

* It was a tragic irony that chose this city for one of the cruellest massacres in history of people
taking refuge in a church.

The Tent and the Canopy

A tent is a portable shelter and therefore, though an individual tent may be used again and again, each separate erection is essentially temporary. Its earliest use may well have been by the hunters of the Old Stone Age. As far as we know nomadic peoples have always used tents: the Jews of the Old Testament and their contemporaries, Indians of the American continent, Arabs of today. Tents have been small and made of hides, large and made of cloth. They have been minimal, stretched on a tripod, or large like a marquee or a circus tent, with enormous poles and a vast system of steadying guy-ropes. They have housed kings on the battlefield, big-game hunters on safari, boy scouts on a hike. The purposes they have served range from grave to frivolous, life-preserving to playful, but they do in fact provide a form of protection, and even of housing, and therefore should not be totally overlooked in an inventory of buildings.

In our analysis two influences of the tent have exerted themselves on what we should unhesitatingly accept as architecture proper: the one in the effect that certain types of permanent buildings may have upon us, and the other in temporary buildings that are raised on similar principles. Whether the wagon 13, 14 inspired the wagon-vault* or vice-versa, there is no doubt that certain vaults built of light fabric have a tent-like buoyancy. The timber vaults of some of Wren's churches are examples, while chapter houses and other round and 51 polygonal structures, even of stone, supported by a pier in the centre have this character, which must occur wherever a central support to the roof is found. All pitched roofs have somewhat of the tent quality, and the steeper they are and the more they continue into the wall and share its protective function, the more they simulate the tent. Early cruck construction found in north-west England suggests a tent form in this way. Among recent tendencies in roof design are some which evoke a tent in their folded centralizing fabric. The serrated roof is merely a repetition of the simple pitched roof designed to strengthen it for large

* A third name for the tunnel or barrel vault.

48
49

spans. Although therefore the traditional type of pitched roof is seldom found in contemporary architecture, a type of 'pleated' roof in which the pleats project has been devised. The rigidity caused by the tension set up is thereby close to the tensional principles from which the tent derives its name.

The famous hangars of Orly designed by Freyssinet in 1916 astonished the world by an imaginative suggestion for using a tent effect to cover vaster areas than had hitherto been required, and Buckminster Fuller's geodesic hemispheres have suggested a further possibility. Probably few men are currently devising anything more seminal than Luigi Nervi, whose famous sports stadia 48, 49 present vast shallow domes framed up like tents, presenting this character more particularly by their supports, which ring the cover in the manner of guy-ropes. Another contemporary designer of roofs in tension has been Eduardo Torroja (1899–1961). 'Most of his designs employ folded, undulating or warped shapes.'[26] In the present context it will be enough to mention the grandstand at Zarzuela racetrack near Madrid, built in 1935, where rigidity is procured by fluting, convex above, and cantilevered two ways. Actual tents have been designed in great numbers by the German engineer, Frei Otto, some of them 50 merely awnings, others intricate systems covering enormous areas with series of spikes or curves. Metal standards are used to promote the spikes, and hawsers to hold the tents steady, and by pulling on the carefully shaped fabric, to ensure the resulting imaginative and multifarious range of cover-shapes that he has devised. Avowedly temporary and expensive to erect, the shelters for the 1972 Olympic Games in Munich were intended to have a limited life for a strictly limited function. Whatever debris these breathtaking tents leave, they are relatively easy to remove without creating the shadow-cities and ghost-towns that other Olympic centres have been left with. Otto is doing something new. It is impossible to assess its potential. But it may spawn something that will be a solution to our problem of rapid obsolescence. His designs may prove one of the most important avenues of thinking to be followed since Le Corbusier. And it is certainly one of the most beautiful, if beauty can be demonstrated.

The tent is enclosed and supports itself. A canopy is essentially a shelter (ritual or real) and is usually supported by some other means. A tent is in tension, held usually by guy-ropes. A canopy is usually suspended. However a canopy may have side flaps which can be attached or let down, and it may be raised from the ground on a frame, while a tent may have its sides rolled up and be erected without the use of posts. So they merge, and are classified here according to their chief function or character.

If all roofs are to a certain extent tents, then all ceilings are canopies to a certain extent, but it may be said that certain Gothic vaults in particular have the effect of canopy rather than structural effort, and this is perhaps particularly true of Late English vaulting, where the structural intention of the thirteenth century, for example, has been totally lost. Instead we have a decoratively woven canopy, like that at King's College Chapel at Cambridge, borne high above us on vertical shafts spraying out at the top to bear it, its function appearing as solely ceremonial as the canopy carried over an oriental prince. Before this, at Chartres for example, a canopy was carved in stone over the head of each portal figure. Suggesting medieval *aediculae* they nevertheless hang over the figures, no doubt offering actual protection to the fabric of the statue, but also defining the 'cylinder' in which the figure and its base are, as it were, contained. This usage of a canopy as space-defining occurs in the quite different situation of Ghana, where the traditional state umbrellas of the Ashanti ruler play this 'architectural' rôle as well as symbolizing various attributes with which he is associated.[27]

Not space-defining, for the height is usually too great for us to relate it to the floor, are cupolas, referred to earlier in this context, especially when used in groups or series. Of Santa Sophia, J. Arnott Hamilton writes, 'The stupendous dome and soaring vaults hang over the vast extent of nave like the canopy of heaven',[28] and although the single dome, especially when bedded upon continuous walls may be likened, as we have done, to a beehive, there is no doubt that domes on pendentives do often present a lightness, and even billowing quality, that suggests suspension rather than compressive weight. The domes of St. Mark's in Venice, aided perhaps by the dark golds and blues of mosaic, which often appear so like brocades and other rich cloths, seem certainly to hang, though heavily, over the cruciform church. Less weighty in appearance, but structurally similar, are the vaults of Romanesque churches in western France, which are obtained by the use of a series of cupolas. St. Front at Périgueux was

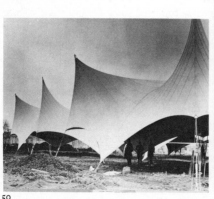

50   51

built about the same time as St. Mark's, and has the same Greek Cross plan
covered by five domes. The whitish stone, which remains the only finish,
probably accounts for the lighter effect. This is found too in other churches of
the region, which have often a single long nave supporting cupolas, whose rôle
here is certainly that of a canopy, even when the domes are expressed externally, usually with a cap of protective tiling.

In modern 'shell' construction where roof and ceiling are combined in the
same cover the shape of the structure will decide whether tent or canopy is
suggested to the viewer. Perhaps the suspended roof will seem most nearly to
approach a canopy, especially when this is thought of in its old simple sense of a
cloth on posts, like a baldacchino. The suspension bridge is an early example of
this kind of structure: its use for cover had to wait until later for full development. One of the earliest usages as such seems to have been at the Raleigh
Arena, North Carolina, in 1952–3.[29] It takes a saddle shape, which has since
become very popular for this type of roof. A later example of suspended roof was
used at the Dulles Airport, by Saarinen, supported on a 'skeleton' structure,
and interesting roofs hanging from supporting posts appeared at the Olympic
arenas at Tokyo in 1961–4, designed by Kenzo Tange. Particularly the smaller
of the two pavilions here recalls a tent. It is circular in plan and the roof 'of a
prestressed steel net on which there are attached welded and painted steel
plates'[30] hangs from a single reinforced concrete 'mast'. The constructional
system is well in evidence, the great supporting cables spiralling down in a
sweep to be anchored in concrete.

The Shell and the Spiral

A shell is a hollow container with gently sloping sides and subtle irregularities
that adapt it to the exclusive use of the organism that occupies it.* The type of a
shell is the Coquille St. Jacques (the scallop) but we do not have to have a
specific variety. The kind of building that comes to mind when one thinks of a
shell is the auditorium, whether covered or not, for the principle of the shell can
be extended to include either background or cover. The first great example was
of course the Greek theatre, or even earlier perhaps the less developed 'theatral p126
place' of the Minoans.

By general consent the theatre of Epidaurus represents the epitome of this

---

* Except for such freaks as the Hermit Crab which, like man, is happy in a shelter originally
meant for someone else.

genre, a fold in the hills selected carefully, and then equally carefully hollowed out and tiered to form the more-than-semicircular auditorium around the large flat circular orchestra, with the platform and background buildings partly concealing the landscape below. The clarity and precision of the superimposed circles of seats held poised in the hollow hill exerts a strong visual stimulation. Though the seats are almost totally concealed when a crowd fills the theatre the human units follow the shape determined by the structure to form in their turn a group of people surely more formally held than in any other setting.

This system of seating people about a spectacle has many variations. Contemporary with the theatre in Greece is the somewhat less dramatic stadium, where more space is naturally allocated to the performers, and the spectators are more spread out around the far larger area.

In default of natural slopes and hollows to provide auditoria, these have been constructed out of masonry, spectacularly in the amphitheatres of the Romans, of which the most considerable was the Colosseum in Rome. The sloping sides of this huge shell were supported by a honeycomb of masonry, arched in structure and arranged both parallel to and normal to the elliptical boundary. Below the floor level of the arena lay a system of dens for the animals awaiting their turn in the ring, and the watching crowd of 50,000 was protected from them by a high wall encircling the arena. This system was the ancestor of the bull-ring, which is circular instead of elliptical but serves a similar purpose. And in fact everywhere in the contemporary world are auditoria of varying shapes based on the structural and plan arrangements of the Greeks and Romans. Sometimes the shell is closed or partly closed with a membranous roof, which may be acoustically treated, continuing the analogy of this type of container.

The 'shell structure' in today's parlance refers to a type of roof or cover, and is so named because of its curved contours which make possible an extreme thinness of material. With this the analogy is often closer to the egg-shell than the scallop, and is included in the 'tent and canopy' section because of its rôle as cover. The 'shells' here reviewed are hollow containers, usually unroofed or partly roofed. Many 'shells' are found, as has been noted, as auditoria, used in combination with flat or pit-shaped adjuncts such as playing fields, stadia, or swimming baths.

A shell which perhaps of all the genre most closely upholds the analogy is the Campo of Siena, a piazza almost exactly following the contours of a large shell, and containing at its deepest part the sculptured form of a scallop. It fans out from an almost straight flat base across which stretches the Palazzo Pubblico to an upper terrace now largely occupied by restaurants, but originally fringed by palazzi of the fourteenth century. It must be one of the most attractive leisure places in Europe now that it has (in accordance with widespread new policy in Italy) been cleared of traffic, particularly parked vehicles. Its character has emerged of positive enclosure and definition, suggesting in fact something of the buoyancy of a shell afloat. In 1419 Jacopo della Quercia completed his Fonte Gaia, as the central feature of the Campo which has something of the waiting quality of a theatral place, not surely induced so much by the event of the annual Palio, as by its having once been the forum of the Roman city, and thus in early times being used for entertainment and display.

Shells that do not fall into the group represented by the scallop, are often of a spiral shape, an arrangement which has not often served the requirements of a whole building—though this has happened. An early type was the Assyrian Ziggurat, a monument square on plan and with a continuous ramp mounting it on the four sides. In Iraq is the spiral tower of Samarra, eleven centuries old and this time circular in plan, which, according to two of Bruegel's paintings was the shape of the Tower of Babel. It was also the form proposed by Tatlin 53 for his monument to the Soviets which was never erected. This was planned as a metal construction and has always been regarded as one of the important examples of Constructivist design in the field of sculpture. It has that equivocal station between sculpture and architecture so often found in monuments, and can be considered perhaps as a poetic latter-day Eiffel Tower (though not 41 mountable). The earliest sketches made by Le Corbusier of Chandigarh suggest that he envisaged the cone of the Assembly Chamber as having an external 43 ramp, though this feature was later omitted.

The spiral is more often found in an invert form, of which the obvious use is as a staircase. This often occupies a type of tower, or specially constructed stair well, but in its more magnificent appearances may be built as a more or less open structure. A great staircase of this type is the one at the Château of Chambord where the complexity is increased by the fact that it is a double helix 54 of which the two flights remain parallel and do not meet.

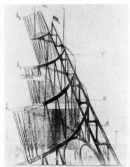

52   53

Perhaps an even more famous stair is the slightly earlier one at the Château of Blois. This is a simpler spiral, but being constructed in its own tower attached to one side to the main building (of François I) makes, perhaps, a more considerable architectural impact. Moreover the sides are open and the stair visible as it rises through three storeys. It is lavishly decorated and is reputed to have owed something to Leonardo da Vinci, who died in France in 1519.

Many open spiral stairs have been of great beauty, especially where the diameter has been of a size to provide views of the staircase as a whole, and where the cantilevered effect adds a fanlike quality to the flights. A notable example of this is at the Queen's House, at Greenwich, but there must be many stairways of distinction built in this manner.

There are basically three types of spiral stair: those supported both by a central support and by the external structure, those supported on the central post alone, and those supported externally only, and thus being open down the centre of the spiral. Historic modern stairs of the centrally supported type were those designed for the Deutscher Werkbund group at the Cologne exhibition of 1914, by Walter Gropius. This must have been the first time spiral staircases rose within glass walls. Open spirals have been used as car ramps and are familiar now in parking garages.

A spiral that has aroused notice in our day is the Guggenheim Museum in
55 New York by Frank Lloyd Wright. Here the spiral is exploited as a path from which the collection may be seen. It has attracted much praise and equal blame. It forces a continuous movement forward on the spectator which is not always greatly to be desired in a display situation, as it tends to emphasize, along with the movement past, the temporary nature of the experience. History is certainly temporal, and so are many of the visual arts, like ballet. Whether one wants to

54   55

emphasize the timeless or the historical in the visual arts would no doubt be a factor in one's approval or non-approval of the Frank Lloyd Wright arrangement. In 1931 Le Corbusier had produced his project for the Museum of Unlimited Growth, a museum of modern art based on a rectilinear spiral and not multi-storeyed like the later building of Wright. Set in a large park it was part of his general programme of possible standardization and multiplication of the unit. But before then, in 1938, he had projected an actual spiral ziggurat for the Musée Mondial at the 'Mundaneum' for the League of Nations. Whatever the nature of the rooms or spaces served by a spiral, the form itself must always imply movement.

Platform and Place

The user of caves and tents comes to terms with his environment; the maker of terraces comes to grips with it. A terrace may be either cut out of a slope or built up from it; either way results in a platform, and man, for his formal business, prefers a series of levels to a series of slopes. It may be protested that a platform can never be architecture in its own right, but it is so intimately related to architecture, so basically and in so many ways that, like some of the other forms we have considered (the beehive, the tunnel) it becomes an important determinant to the character of a building, and should come in at least for a brief analysis.

The raising of a platform to define the floor level of a building was so important in Greece and Rome that it has persisted through history, from the stylobate (a platform meant to raise the Greek temple to an eminence above   10 the common footway) and the podium of the equally elevated temple of the   22 Romans, to the high base on which it seemed only proper to the men of the humanist Renaissance that churches should stand.   12, 25

A platform seemed to the ancient world a necessary definition of a place where people should stand or sit for various occasions. The stoa, a covered colonnade reached by steps, was a necessary part of any Greek town. On this philosophers spoke to their students, or citizens met in discussion. It is easy to view it as an architectural type because of its peristylar nature, but this formality is not rare. The Romans made use of rostra for speakers who wished to address a crowd. These could be considered a parallel to the logeion, or speak-   p126 ing platform of the Greek theatre. Stages and platforms for similar purposes can be found everywhere today. The dais is a form of this; in the medieval hall the section of the floor which was higher than the rest, enabling the lord of the manor to sit 'higher' than his household, a formality still found in the conventional 'high table'.

The use of reinforced concrete has enormously promoted the use of the platform as an architectural character. The layers of floor themselves are now platforms, since they can now project beyond the screen or glass walls to form levels or 'decks'. The split-level house is nothing but an exploitation of the space excitement of different levels of platform. The roof garden and penthouse are another instance.

One of the historically most significant types of platform, that of the railway station, gives signs of falling into obsolescence. Here, often with imaginative use of the Canopy, was something vital to the late nineteenth century. And when we come to the harbour and the pier we have a form of platform so antique as to warrant the title of *terra firma* itself. Are these on the way out? They seem to be given scant attention today.

From the platform it is appropriate to pass to a consideration of the 'place', which I mean easily, either in the French or English sense; any place deliberately shaped for human concourse, not *built* but arranged as an interval between buildings, which thus allow their external faces to become, as it were, the interior decoration of the 'place'. However, in its architectural function as an important environmental entity it is never merely a gap: it is always purposefully defined. It is at its most negative a clearing, and at its most positive an enclosure. In a forest a clearing is made by cutting down trees and removing undergrowth: among human habitations the same effect is achieved, not necessarily by pulling down buildings, but by not putting them up. Many town and village 'squares' are in this sense clearings—unbuilt-on areas. The agora in a Greek town was often this. The market square in a medieval village was often just a space, *left*. Bombed areas have often been 'left' as parks or gardens; empty lots have been planted instead of being built over. The Roman Agora in Athens has been literally cleared to define again the 'place' of ancient times. Slum clearance sometimes provides a place for leisure or communal activity.

An enclosure is rather different. Where a stoa was provided on one or more sides of an agora in a Greek city (like Priene), or a forum in Rome was deliberately created with its flanking basilica and libraries; when a town or part of a town is planned around a piazza, or a village around a green, whenever buildings are deliberately arranged in relation to a square, or a circus, or a shaped area of any sort, we have an enclosure.

Both of the above, and a range of areas between the two, inasmuch as they are deliberately instigated, are 'places'. We have a wide range from which to choose our reference. The Zulu (especially the Ndebele tribe) modelling his present-day village somewhat upon that of the white man, builds a walled-in area adjacent to his house which he calls his *lapa*.* We may start with this, for surely the first extension to the built environment is that nearest to the habitation. In classical times and lands such an area was a courtyard, usually an integral part of the house itself. Then came the agora or forum, the 'courtyard' of the town as a whole; later the plateia, the piazza, the plaza, the *place*. In northern countries less congenial to open air lounging, the public square may have shown a brisker life: markets tend to be covered and therefore buildings in a proper sense. The open space was that before the cathedral or other important public building.

Let us look at the different character of some of the great 'places' of history.

The Greek temenos: this was a zone for temples, and though there is some controversy as to whether we have a right to regard it as other than a negative space between the temples within its walls, the fact that there were walls implies in itself that the temenos was looked upon as an area, an architectural entity in fact, containing the temples, and certainly with some considerable formal treatment. If we take the sanctuary at Sunium, near Athens, as an example, we find demonstrable sophistication, and even subtlety, in the layout determining progression from the propylaea to the altar before the temple of Poseidon. The 'classic' quality of a gatehouse or propylaea is not only to provide a possible check-point where admittance can be controlled, but a halting place where the visitor will be prepared mentally for what he will be introduced to beyond it. At an Egyptian valley temple, like that of Chephren, which was the entrance to p120 the pyramid tomb of the king's funeral cortège, it is thought that the body (and perhaps certain of its attendants) underwent purification rites before it was allowed to proceed. All gateways imply a halt as well as a passage, and certainly the propylaea of Greek sanctuaries narrow and enclose the environment after the visitor's approach before opening up and releasing him into the wider but formally controlled space of the temenos. Here he is in a consecrate ambience, and his further activities will be confined to those proper to the temple precincts.

A similar though less formally designed situation is found with a cathedral close such as Salisbury or Wells, where the great west front dominates the stretch of sward before it, and to a lesser extent in cathedral squares in France and Italy, where the distracting presence of shops and other places of business lowers the conditioning potency of the church. Perhaps Italian designers of the seventeenth century felt this falling away of the sense of the presence of the church, when, partly in response to urgent appeals emanating from the Council

---

* There is no exact English translation for *lapa*, which denotes only his yard, in fact defines his 'place'.

of Trent, they began to give greater attention to the setting (as well as the decorative content) of churches. The massive colonnade enclosing the elliptical piazza before St. Peter's is one of the most potent of these controls, appearing as it does on ceremonious occasions to provide a Place for half of Rome. Other seventeenth-century piazze of Rome are the Piazza Navona (though its effect is secular rather than religious) and the theatrical arrangement of the Piazza S. Ignazio, where the fronts of the buildings opposite the church have been arranged in an elaborate symmetrical curve. Baroque interest in ornate arrangement has given us the Piazza di Spagna with the great flow of twisting stair, and one of the finest of them all (though much earlier) we must not overlook Michelangelo's splendid Capitol, the trapezoidal piazza formed by the twin museums, and the Senatore, which still speaks (as Georgina Masson reminds us[31]) as the *Senatus Populusque Romanus*.

In a land of delicate and splendid Places two stand out as matchless. The first is the complex of Piazza and Piazzetta in Venice, 'without an equal in the world' says the *Blue Guide* to Northern Italy. It is impossible to do justice to this in description. The piazza is in itself the Piazza San Marco. But in fact nothing in the square, not even the campanile is anywhere near contemporary with the cathedral, which was built in the eleventh century though it has suffered restorations of the sixteenth and later. The campanile was first built at the end of the ninth century; much rebuilt in the sixteenth it collapsed in 1902 and was rebuilt for the second time shortly before the First World War (1912). The buildings on either side of the slightly tapering piazza are of the sixteenth century. They carried the residence of the Procurators over a grand arcade

56

running around the whole square and backed now by the shops of jewellers and glass or linen merchants. At the west end a church by Sansovino was replaced in the nineteenth century by a building which forms the termination of the square and the main entrance to it. The square is paved with marble, upon which pigeons are fed and orchestras play ceaselessly. Though the angle of the north walls and the continuity of the arcaded backing of the piazza serve to throw the interest always in the direction of the glittering façade of the cathedral, this alone would not contrive the actual nobility and interest of the setting. It is its extension at a right angle into what is called the Piazzetta that raises it to its summit of grandeur and enchantment.

To the south of San Marco and giving continuity to it is the Palace of the Doges, opposite which is Sansovino's Libreria Vecchia. The Piazzetta lies between these grand and brilliantly sunlit buildings to the quays on the edge of the Grand Canal which provide a frontage of what must be half a mile of jetties and moorings along a broad promenade. Defining the evasive border between Piazzetta and Molo have stood, since the twelfth century, two monolithic columns with spreading capitals bearing the Lion of St. Mark ('wings modern' says the *Blue Guide*) and the first Patron of Venice, St. Theodore. Although these must antedate the buildings that define the piazza, and although this could not have been planned in its entirety at any one time, so felicitous is the result that it forms a complex remembered as a unified totality. This is perhaps an important thinking-point in a definition of architectural aesthetics. Since architecture in its most important viewing (i.e. as environment) must needs operate as a continuum, however jerkily propelled, one can think of it as pre-

57

planned only in relatively small portions. The quality of good architecture may well lie in its capacity for being caught up in the flexion and integrated with it. No vast system of planning should be continued simply because it was planned, if any aspects of the planning become obsolete before completion. (This has been the tragedy of Liverpool Cathedral: the mode of architectural thinking that produced its design was obsolete before the building was begun.) This may be a reason why gardens are so often more successful than houses, because people accept and arrange for their changing.

2   The second place for which supremacy must be claimed is the happily named Campo dei Miracoli at Pisa. The miracles may well be chiefly architectural. Uniquely in Italy (I believe) the cathedral and its related buildings, the baptistry, the bell-tower, and the Camposanto (or enclosed cemetery) are set out on a level lawn traversed by stone paths. The circular baptistry was set (nearly 100 years later) west of the church on its main east–west axis, but not so near it as in any way to spoil the approach to the west front. The Camposanto, still later by more than another hundred years, lies to the north, and forms with its outer wall a firm linking definition to the main approach path between the two other

15   buildings, and a little south and east is the campanile, the 'Leaning Tower', described on page 64. An airview shows splendidly the relations of these four buildings, but moving about and among them also provides a visual experience without precise parallel. The facing is all of that Tuscan marble which is compounded of adjacent pieces and strips of gentle colour with white. The whole glints softly in the Italian light and is set off by the grassed area which, with the more specific white paths, acts as an integrating plane.

All adequate and touching places are not large in dimensions. Pienza is one of many Italian hill towns that show charming examples. The Piazza Pio II reflects the Florentine quattrocento, and owes its character to Bernardo Rossellino, architect to Pius II Piccolomini whose birthplace it was and who gave it his name in 1462. The Palazzo Piccolomini forms one side of the square, with its well-head at one corner, the cathedral another, flanked by glimpses of the spectacular view over the surrounding plain. Opposite the church are the loggia of the Palazzo Communale and the tables of a tavern. Housed in the buildings on the east side, which complete the little square, is the museum. In France too we may single out of many the town of Conques, with its famous Pilgrimage Church of Sainte-Foy. The façade of this church, with its marvellous Romanesque tympanum of the Last Judgement, forms a whole side of the small square levelled out of the hillside.

Every house cannot have its own garden, but town houses often have, as in many a London square, access to the planted area which they surround. Though these 'gardens' cannot be exactly described as architecture, the provision for them certainly is urban architecture of a most important kind, an aspect of town planning which is fundamentally an extension of architecture. 'Landscape Architecture' is not often referred to by that name today, but was a significant concept of the eighteenth and nineteenth centuries. The planning of the 'Great House' in England or the Château in France included as a matter of course the layout of the court, the formal garden with its parterres, fountains, and reflecting pools, and its surrounding parklands and woods. There is no precise point at which the formal terraces meeting the formal or even informal gardens can be said to mark the 'end' of the architecture. The 'Place' is not necessarily formal, though if it is to be considered architecture it is always defined and related to adjacent buildings and natural forms.

Nor is it, by the same token, always urban. The theatre of a Greek city and the areas connected with it were often outside the walls, as was the temenos. The sanctuaries of Delphi and Olympia were independent of their neighbouring towns. In spite of the eighteenth-century horror of uncultivated nature, country houses were often set only in the relative civilization of their own 'Place' and perhaps miles from other like refuges, though agricultural cultivation where possible made tolerable the wider zone of countryside. The English landed gentry always took this fairly well, but the worst thing that could happen to a nobleman of the eighteenth century in France was to be excluded from the Royal Court and to have to go to his own estate in the country, which, however grand it may be was banishment in terms of the civilities of Versailles.

In early times when all the world was remote and inimical the mere defining of a 'Place' had enormous meaning. In this context an arrangement like Stonehenge shows the total significance of architecture. Neither shelter nor container Stonehenge, nevertheless, grandly defines a zone, and this physical grandiloquence leaves us in no doubt of its numinous rôle, though its actual function remains obscured by time. Investigators have demonstrated that the positioning of the stones reflected astronomical calculations, but there is a range of possible uses to which that esoteric knowledge could have been put. Whatever informative directions the stones marked out implied knowledge arrived at in other ways, and could have been passed on more simply. As with the possible mathematics involved in the Egyptian pyramids, this is not the motivation of the structure as such, but only a motivation of its positioning. The science serves the architecture and not vice versa. We pause here in the presence of great art.

III

The Plan as the Generator

Le plan est le générateur.
Sans plan, il y a désordre, arbitraire.
Le plan porte en lui l'essence de la sensation.

Le Corbusier, Vers une Architecture.

Aesthetic of the Plan

The architect is first a planner. If he cedes this rôle not only he but architecture is lost because no one else is trained for it. A plan may be copied or derived or adapted. In vernacular building the space-unit may be so simple, or have become so much of a tradition, that it is used with little variation; but architecture of any individual merit concerns the disposal of space and solid in relations determined by the architect. He designates this largely by means of his plan.

To an architect a plan is a drawing, and the term is rarely used in any other sense. There are as many plans as there are floors to a building. If simply 'the plan' is referred to it is usually the plan at ground floor level (called the 'ground plan' by art historians but not by architects) or it is the first 'living' floor. In single space buildings like churches or halls there is one main plan, though one may have additional plans as 'at gallery level'.

A plan then is basically a floor layout. But it is a little more complicated than this. By usage all doorways and other openings are shown on the plan, and windows too, however high the sills may be above the floor. Often the construction of a vaulted ceiling is indicated on the plan, usually by means of dotted lines. A plan layout, or a site plan, shows the building in relation to neighbouring structures. Here fountains, gardens, trees, steps, statues, altars, benches, streams, or anything else may be indicated that is relevant to the setting and appearance of the building in question. It has been suggested that the plan is a view of the floor, but it is not quite this; it is not a view of the building at all in the physical sense. An elevation is a straightforward description of an outer wall. A section is a view *into* the building with a wall or walls stripped away. But a plan is almost totally conceptual: it is the architect's view of his building. It is our view of the architect's intention.

Plans are drawn for different purposes. They form, together with elevations and sections, the working drawings which are given to the builder to instruct him in his procedure. These are usually heavily dimensioned and annotated and accompanied by a detailed specification. Another kind of drawing that may be prepared is what is sometimes known as a 'black-and-white'. This emphasizes solid in relation to space, and is the kind of drawing an architect may use for publication, or for his own satisfaction, or to show clients, or future clients. It is also the kind of drawing made of buildings already in existence (where instructions are not needed) and it is of course the kind that is, where possible, used here. Both sections and elevations are an attempt to project what can be seen in the building itself. The plan however has no counterpart in the material sense, and describes a concept.

R. G. Collingwood attempted to define the zone of existence of works of art.[1]

He would not admit the necessity of material existence, but considered the work as purely conceptual, having its being (to simplify the theory) only in the imagination or 'mind' of the artist. Literature, for example, has no existence in space. It is apprehended by the senses of sound and sight through the presentation of symbols. It could be offered as a criticism of Collingwood that he is misled in trying to equate those arts whose manifestations do occupy space,, or which cannot be substituted or presented by symbols, too closely with literature. Does an area of pictorial composition exist in the artist's mind before execution as completely as does a phrase or sentence in the writer's? Perhaps Collingwood means only that the 'desert island' artist, having completed his work, may tear it up without destroying it; that it will continue to exist as long as he does. Continuity beyond the lifetime of an artist must imply his having communicated it to someone else or (and this is surely an important point in relation to works of art) his having left it in a material form.

Decision on this delicate point rests on the part played by communication in the activity of the artist. What remains in his mind only is possibly rather than potentially communicable, but even when the artwork has been put forward in a material form, what is communicated to the 'ideal spectator'* may well have no material existence, the 'material' merely helping to transmit. This is obvious in the case of the written word; not so happily taken in the case of painted canvas or chiselled marble.

Even if we accept, in despite of Collingwood (but with one eye on him), that a painting is not made until it is painted, its existence is a fairly simple situation: it was made by the hand of the artist, obviously in his lifetime, and will last as a work of art as long as it materially exists. The metaphysics (if we may call it that) of architecture is very much more complicated. Let us first accept that a building is something that is in fact built. But the men who lay the bricks do not create it much more than a typesetter creates literature; and yet there is a difference. Eric Gill would have said several arts are involved.[2] You may have a good book badly printed (or vice-versa) because the art of book production is not the same as that of writing, but you cannot have a good *building* badly *built* because you are talking, or seem to be talking, of the same art (as you could not have a good painting badly painted). What you could have is a good architectural design badly built. But is even this what we mean? It would seem to indicate that 'architecture' means only preliminary designing (and thus vindicate the Collingwood approach) but in fact we admire the building in its actuality, we think of architecture as designing with materials; we are liable to consider the delicacy of carving as much a part of the Parthenon as the proportions and disposition of the columns and entablature.

* A term I use to suggest a person who totally comprehends.

With buildings of certain periods, such as the Middle Ages, the material fabric is the building. Even in modern times it tends to be what the architect has achieved in terms of available materials that impresses or moves us. Sometimes the architect has been badly served by his executants, so that the results are shoddy. To a great extent such a building is, whatever its designing, a failure. Shakespeare is not negated to the same extent by bad production, nor Beethoven by bad playing. This is because, by the nature of their art, they may be repeated many times. They may also both be known by reading. Whether a music score can convey to the reader anything approaching the actual timbre and power of an orchestra, we must leave to the experts to tell us. Certainly as far as drama and poetry are concerned many, perhaps most, scholars prefer the script to the performance. It excludes, they claim, the human imperfections of the interpretative go-between, the actor. It leaves them with the pure dicta of the Master, which they may peruse and interpret in their own way (and at their own pace). The construction of a building is not a 'performance' in the same sense, and is to only a slight extent an 'interpretation'. However because there is some margin for misinterpretation, the architect's personal supervision of a building is regarded as important. Thus we do not forget that Rossellino, not Alberti himself, supervised the building of the Rucellai palace in Florence; that Sant'Andrea in Mantua was largely carried out by another architect, Luca Fancelli; that Michelangelo did not live to see his dome built at St. Peter's (it was constructed 'after his design'); that Wren was the only architect to work on St. Paul's, though it took almost his lifetime to build. When the architect is not present considerable variation from what he intended may creep in. No one can be sure that it is his work, that it has been made with his approval. Also it has material existence. There is no repeat performance. It is a material object, existing in space.

But it does also exist in time, like music or literature, though it does not move. It is the spectator who must move if he wants to have seen it wholly. For see it as a whole in one impact he cannot, however long a time is allowed. There is no one place from which he can apprehend it totally. To a certain extent this is true too of sculpture in the round, especially large sculpture, though the time required to view it from all relevant points is always much less. Even in a single room the spectator has to change position to see it, and when there are many rooms the time factor becomes highly significant. The thorough investigation of large buildings like Versailles, inside and out, together with their dependencies (such as the Trianons) can be too much for a continuous process, and, like a novel, has to be set aside for completion another day.

But something of the total intention of the architect can be read from the plan, and there are many of us who would rather sit down with a plan, if we want to understand a building, than a photograph, or even a set of photographs, which, unless the building is very simple, tell us little indeed about it until we have studied the plan. Nor is the communication afforded by the plan confined to information, even information about the architect's visual or aesthetic intentions. 'The plan holds in itself,' wrote Le Corbusier in 1923, 'the essence of sensation,'[3] and though perhaps the connotation of 'sensation' is not quite the same in English as it is in French, it is clear that we are to regard the plan as being evocative and moving in itself. In his consideration of the plan as the 'generator' Le Corbusier implied (and has always been understood as implying) more than merely that the plan is the key to the zoning and relations of the building. It emerges in his phrase as determining (and therefore afterwards powerfully reflecting) its shape and space relations, but also its genre, its muscularity, its virility, its total character as architecture. Furthermore in this rôle it may carry within itself that peculiar potency which gives rise to what traditionally has been called the 'aesthetic' response. It would be going too far to suggest that it was merely the relations of lines on paper (like an abstract painting) that evoked a response: clearly the ability to 'read' a plan at all implies a thorough understanding of what each part of the drawing represents, yet it would not be true either to maintain that the aesthetic response to a plan was solely a response to the visualization of what the plan implies in terms of the building as actually constructed. (This argument will be supported and exemplified in the analyses of plans that follow.)

The plan may be considered in a sense as the 'spoor' of a building. Just as an elephant will leave a large and positive imprint of its foot, and a small antelope a delicate hoof-print, so a structure of heavy stone will show in its plan a far bolder silhouette than a light structure of glass and metal. Carrying the footprint analogy a little further we may say that it is not only size and weight that are indicated but other characters of the building; as with animals the marks indicate hoof or pad, and by distribution, speed of travel, and thus possibly state of mind from tranquillity to terror. Often one may be confronted with a plan of an unfamiliar or still projected work, but one will usually recognize immediately the genre to which it broadly belongs and its approximate date. This knowledge will in its turn qualify our interpretation and reaction, so that it is almost inconceivable that an experienced viewer should read the plan in an unrelated imaginative vacuum. What is far more likely is that we shall be reading the plan of a building already familiar, either in itself or in its environment, and that the plan will therefore play its part as summation, or even consummation, of our experience of the work of architecture.

We have no architects' drawings from antiquity though drawings there must have been. Vitruvius refers to drawings included in his *Books* to explain certain constructional methods, and although it is likely, from the precise nature of some of these explanations, that the architect of his day was more closely connected with the actual process of building than he normally is today, it would have been almost impossible to achieve precision in the vast scale of many buildings of antiquity without small explanatory drawings, even if they were sketches merely, and not to scale. The sophistication and competence of wall-decoration, at Pompeii for example, indicates that precision drawing as such would have presented no problems to draftsmen of the first century B.C. and probably even earlier.

The Romans favoured symmetry, which may have been partly for the effect of the general massing of such buildings evenly on either side of a central approach, and partly the pleasure of symmetrical patterning on the plan. The mirror image about a central axis of variously shaped courts, halls and, later, stairways and flanking wings and pavilions, stayed with architects who had revived the Roman vocabulary of design, into the nineteenth century and after, rendering sterile such perpetuations as competition drawings for the *Prix de Rome* and ultimately helping to make the term 'academic' a derogatory one. Though we may read these plans as two-dimensionally disposed, however, there is no reason to conclude that the designer was not visualizing the various parts of the building, quite properly, as three-dimensional spaces. Structure in classical building was fairly straightforward during the eighteenth century. Indeed we have criticized just this rather lazy acceptance as being a major factor of the architect's having lost a certain prestige, and certainly precedence, to the engineer.

Bruno Zevi has suggested that the cult of the plan was a dangerous aesthetic assumed especially by followers of Le Corbusier,[4] and there is no doubt that approval of his free-plan constructional system does transfer easily to a recognition of the admired qualities in the plans themselves, which may certainly lead to a sketching convention sometimes appearing to suppress structural and other detail and leaving the merest indication of supporting and screening systems. The clarity of articulation in some of his larger projects, like those for the League of Nations (1927) or the Palace of the Soviets (1931) fostered in some of his admirers a development of plan-indication that was little more than a zoning diagram, and probably got most of its response from a recognition of a brilliant planning technique and the symbols that refer to it. Nevertheless one cannot really omit the factor of an 'aesthetic of the plan', nor even wish to do so. The plan is the architect's thinking aloud about a volume construction. As he sketches he is defining space relations which are already real in his mind but become more whole as he defines them with his pencil. Eventually, so deeply is his special language understood, the drawing becomes not merely an explanation or an instruction but an imaginative communication in its own right. To a person understanding the language conveyed by the conventional symbols of that communication the reading of a plan is as direct as the reading of words, certainly as direct as the reading of a mathematical statement or a musical score by one sufficiently acquainted with the conventions used. Thus a plane of communication is established involving neither that understanding of plan-drawing conventions which a builder would translate into his appropriate materials, nor an abstract pattern such as would be found in, say, a modern graphic work, but something between the two; for although the architect has perfectly intended that the builder shall understand the conventions so that he can get on with the job, he also intends the disinterested viewer to find that complete aesthetic statement to which we have referred.

We have suggested that there are qualities in an architectural work that can only be perfectly apprehended by reading the plan. One is internal symmetry, especially on a large scale, for although one can sometimes 'feel' it, it is only possible to verify by a study of the plan. In the same way a lack of symmetry, except in the immediate space in which the viewer is standing, is difficult and sometimes impossible to read internally. Another thing often impossible to gauge in a complex building is the relation of its parts, and even of adjoining rooms. A third quality, only possible to see in the most transparent of struc-tures, is the structural system itself and the relations of space to solid. Again personal impact will reveal certain important emotive and aesthetic qualities, such as the difference in space-occupation between the piers of Gothic and High Renaissance buildings.[5] More subtle factors, such as the movement intended by the architect for the viewer, or the vistas themselves, are sometimes experienced empirically but comprehended perfectly only after scrutiny of the plan.

Factors such as the above, which the plan renders comprehensible, are easily demonstrated. What is less easy to define is that sense of delight and of direct communication with the designer that can reward the peruser of plans. Plans that are beautiful or meaningful in this sense should not be capable of being projected into an unacceptable whole structure, for the reason suggested above, that the architect is not concerned with a two-dimensional design, but a totality of which the plan is the indicator. This indicator can therefore not be satisfac-tory unless the project as a whole is satisfactory.

It should be pointed out before we begin our reading of individual plans that what we have referred to as 'aesthetic delight' experienced in the reading of a plan is not necessarily either a recognition of beauty in the simple sense, nor of approval of the individual work, though it might sometimes be both of these. It is evoked by the same kind of 'apprehension' that we have suggested accompanies acknowledgement of the artwork as an artwork, and especially of the validity of the artist's intention in that work. Thus we may respond to the cave-like character of a building though we do not like caves, or soar with a mounting staircase though we do not like heights. To recognize totally the insubstantial quality of a glass house with minimal supports is not to endorse this as suitable or desirable. The world of art can impinge on every emotion, forcing us to accept an experience of imaginative potency which in every part is not necessarily a pleasant one.

Eighteen Plans: An Exercise in Reading

The Pyramid Temple of Chephren at Giza, 4th Dynasty, Old Kingdom (28–26 century B.C.)

There is an excitement in reading the plans of 'excavated' architecture which is akin to that of exploring a cave itself. There is no relevant façade apart from the entrance. Either the building cannot be seen externally, or what can be seen does not at all indicate the appearance of the interior. This pyramid temple, like most Egyptian buildings, has an exterior shape which is a plain block of construction, square for the valley temple and rectangular for the actual Pyramid Temple, joined by the raking strip of causeway passage. All buildings here have battered walls, making the flat tops slightly smaller in area than the ground covered, though this of course is not visible from the plan.

The valley temple is approached from the river, and in its façade are two doorways, each flanked by sphinxes confronting each other so that those entering pass between them. There is an architectural duality here which may be connected with ritual, like 'in' and 'out' doors, but we do not know. They lead to symmetrically placed hallways which debouch into a common vestibule. From this a relative narrowing occurs before the large T-shaped hall is reached, its roof supported on substantial square piers. Off one wing of the T a set of three chambers branches candelabra-wise from a slender passage. From the other wing, almost casually, a long passage flanked by other passages or cells slants off to become the causeway to the larger temple.

It reaches this in the same informal manner as that in which it had left the valley temple, breaking in, as it were, on to a passage leading off another vestibule-like chamber supported by two piers. From now on we find relentless symmetry, even in the disposing of elements which would not be in view during the progression through the temple. First a broad and shallow hypostyle hall, narrowing in steps towards the neck of another hypostyle hall, this time taking

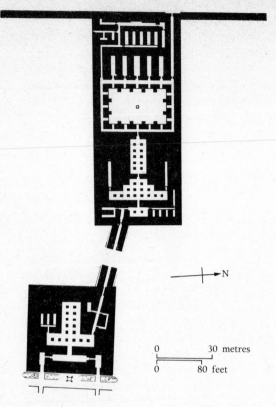

N

0   30 metres
0   80 feet

the direction of the general movement and three-aisled, then (and this is the only break out of the 'cave') a large and obviously unroofed court, surrounded by a covered passage. After this there is no general movement indicated. There is a series of five deeply buried chambers approached through narrow necks from the courtyard ambulatory, and an almost furtive approach to the pyramid. Balancing this an angled narrow passage peters out in a further series of chambers, and perhaps a way out of what has become virtually a maze within the enclosing block.

On plan we thus read a series of larger or smaller chambers and halls linked to each other by narrow passages and necks. If we project ourselves imaginatively into these spaces the sense of enclosure seems oppressive, however large they may be. Standing within them, even imaginatively, we cannot ever be aware of continuity or contiguity, still less of symmetrical disposition or a planned totality. Clearly the designer of these massive complexes of masonry intended them to be secretive and mysterious, impossible to interpret from without, terrifyingly deterrent from within, but in his mind and that of any person thoroughly conversant with the plan methodically set out within the encroaching mass of the structure.

The Great Temple of Rameses at Abu Simbel, 20th Dynasty, New Empire (14 century B.C.)

The pyramid temples were constructed in the Egyptian manner of 'excavation architecture'. This temple is an actual excavation or speos in the cliff face of the Valley of the Kings. It has only one entrance, as can be seen at once from the plan, the wide 'mouth' of the cave cut into the sloping rock and given an extra outward angle to the 'lip' on each side. Two massive pairs of seated portrait figures of Rameses flank the doorway: on plan the extrance seems rather to force its way between them, to pierce into an inner hall, with two rows of heavy piers left standing to support the roof mass. Opposite the entrance a further doorway leads to a series of inner chambers of decreasing size terminating in a small sanctuary. Long rooms, presumably for storage, have been bored into the matrix, but in such a way as hardly to disturb the symmetry of the excavation as it must seem from within, and only revealing their full extent and shape on the plan drawing. The temple narrows as we penetrate into it from the cliff face. This is physically logical for an excavation and builds up gradually the sense of enclosure appropriate to this kind of funerary architecture.

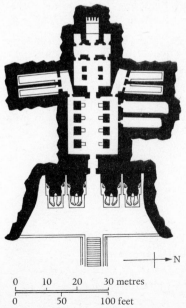

0   10   20   30 metres

0   50   100 feet

The Temple of Khons at Karnak, 20th–21st Dynasty, New Empire (14–13 century B.C.)

The emergence of the Pylon Temple seems to have been roughly contemporary with the excavation of rock temples like Abu Simbel. The similarity of architectural progression from entrance to sanctuary cannot be accidental and would seem to have developed from actual excavation techniques. Thus at Khons we find an architectural approximation to an approach to a face of rock in the two great sloping pylons which characterize all these temples and protect the entrance, while the lack of other exterior façades on the excavated temples is simulated by the blank stretch of thick walling that girdles the temple without in any way revealing its interior character. The inner sanctuary reached after successive reductions in the size of the processional halls is thus embedded in its surrounding chambers and masonry as the sanctuary in the excavated temple is embedded in its earth or rock.

All this is clear on the plan, which usually shows us first (though not at Khons) the relentless rhythm of stone ritual animals directing our feet to the entrance. We are finally marshalled between colossal statues of the Pharaoh, or great obelisks increased in apparent height by the tapering upwards, as are the pylons themselves. We are driven into the passage between the pylons and then partially reprieved by the great court, its centre clearly open to sky and light, its covered sides offering an area of dark and cool which represented for most people the end of their journey to the shrine of the God, for they were not allowed to penetrate further the mysteries of the cult.

For the privileged it was indeed a penetration. The hypostyle hall (H) admitted some light through its slatted windows, but the sides of the hall must have disappeared into darkness. The final sanctuary (S), totally enclosed, and almost totally dark would have to be lit by lamps or torches. Doorways opened off to the sides, for most people inaccessible. The pattern of the forward processional movement, flanked by darkness and mystery, is similar to that of the excavated temples, not only in the layout but, as the plans show us, in architectural intention.

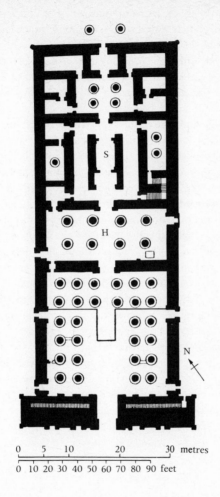

S

H

N

0   5   10   20   30 metres

0 10 20 30 40 50 60 70 80 90 feet

Two Houses at Delos, 2nd century B.C.

One of the factors to bear constantly in mind when reading a plan is the scale. A great temple or palace may cover acres of ground which makes all the more relevant the thickness of supporting walls to the spans to be supported. A private house is a very different problem both structurally and in the disposition of its parts. It is unlikely that there was an architect at hand for these two adjacent houses on the island of Delos, and they follow an established vernacular.

Although the outer walls are of no importance architecturally, they are integral to the house plans in defining the shapes and limits available within which to build, and no space is wasted. Here the narrow and possibly unsavoury streets, forming as they evidently do a public drainage system as well as a passageway between these unpretentious dwellings (though the drains are indicated as running below the street surface), hardly invite windows or more doors than the minimum number possible to open into them. Instead each house relies on its own central court, however small, for air and light. A block was totally built over, and the two houses shown here form part of a block of irregular shape. The rooms all open on to a peristyle, or covered area around the court. The rooms are roughly squared with the outer walls, which results in some irregularity both in the rooms themselves and in the courts. At this intimate scale such imprecise craftsmanship is one of the endearing qualities of vernacular. Both of the houses had shops open to the street, on the same system as that at Pompeii and Herculaneum (both, it will be remembered, also Hellenistic towns). They were evidently single storeyed, and looking at the plans brings us very close to feeling their physical presence. They were not necessarily uncomfortable: one even has a bathroom, though these were rare in Delos, presumably because of the shortage of water.[6] The small formality of the court enhances the sense of enclosure, an attractive feature of small-scale vernacular building.

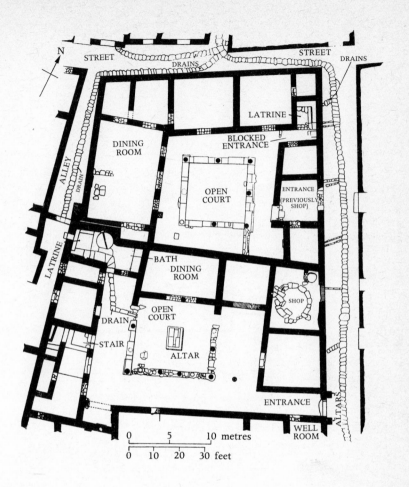

N

STREET

DRAINS

STREET

DRAINS

ALLEY

DRAIN

DINING
ROOM

LATRINE

BLOCKED
ENTRANCE

OPEN
COURT

ENTRANCE
(PREVIOUSLY
SHOP)

LATRINE

BATH
DINING
ROOM

SHOP

DRAIN

OPEN
COURT

STAIR

ALTAR

ENTRANCE

ALTARS

WELL
ROOM

0   5   10 metres

0   10   20   30 feet

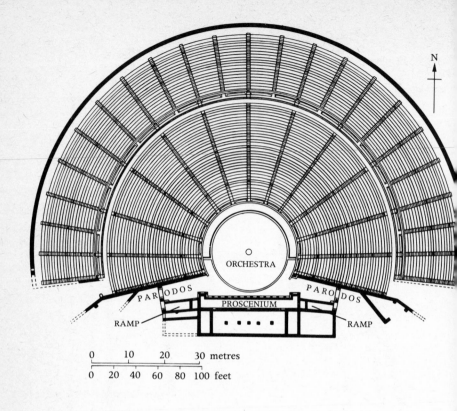

N

ORCHESTRA

PAR ODOS

PROSCENIUM

PAR ODOS

RAMP

RAMP

| 0 | 10 | 20 | 30 metres |

| 0 | 20 | 40 | 60 | 80 | 100 feet |

The Theatre of Epidaurus, 4th century B.C.

The plan of an uncovered building is different from other plans in that it is more nearly an actual view of the building as seen from directly overhead, but since this is not in most cases a practical position for the spectator it tends to remain almost as much an intellectual projection as other plans. In the case of Greek and Roman theatres and amphitheatres the variation in depth from point to point on the plan may be very considerable, so that the plan is a compromise to some extent and not so revealing as an actual view on the site 'looking down' would be. Still there are some things that appear on plan which are not so clearly defined when one is looking down, even here. First of all the clarity of the shape as conceived by the designer is not necessarily apparent or apprehensible to the spectator. The orchestra is a full circle. The auditorium laps round it, not stopping at the rigid geometry of a semi-circle characteristic of the Roman theatre. There is in fact here no sensation of a 'cut' edge, and this is a place evolved directly from, and always with sensitive reference to, the site. The approach-ways to seats in the auditorium show clearly on the plan, which somehow manages to suggest in their tapering, and in the decrease of the number of seats they serve, not only the natural contraction of the circular shape itself towards the centre, but its conical implications. Of course the plan shows the relative complexity of back-stage buildings that the audience does not see—and is intended not to see.

It is not meant to suggest from the above that a plan of Epidaurus, or any other Greek theatre, is any kind of *substitute* for the actual site, even today, or even further, that it could be regarded as superior. This analysis of plans means only to show how they carry forward our awareness of the architectural intention that determines the ultimate structure.

The Baths of Caracalla, 3rd century A.D.

So much has been written of the splendour and luxury of the Roman Baths that the implications of the plan stand out at once. This is made even clearer by the fact that the halls and grand chambers are generally single-spaced areas carrying their own roofing but not a second storey: there is no sign of staircases though there may have been upper floor rooms over the smaller chambers. Restorations show the widely spread arrangement of the plan covering such a vast area (about 270,000 square feet) that even the highest of the great vaulted halls would not have made any impact of verticality. This main block was set in an enclosed area of over a thousand feet square, and properly speaking we should consider this whole domain in our reading of the plan of the baths.

A glance is enough to inform us of the symmetrical arrangement applying to the whole complex. Across the strong central axis which runs south-east/north-west spreads the block of the baths themselves, although 'spreads' is not a good word to describe the tautly-knit inter-relation of its parts. We read first the broadly rectangular shape of the whole, made up of a nearly square area on each side of the axis, on the south-east stretch of which projects the round of the *Caldarium* (C), its thick wedge-shaped piers arranged radially around it, breaking the continuous line of the straight wall by emerging for about two-thirds of its perimeter. From the dense masonry of its piers we may read that they supported a heavy dome (despite its being lightened by the use of *dolia**).

On the central axis moving north-west lies the smaller *Tepidarium* (T), a hall flanked by baths presumably partaking of the heating system devised for the caldarium, and then the high vaulted central hall (H),[7] containing along its

---

* Hollow vessels.

sides cold plunge baths, which, with the two end halls each separated from it by a screen of two columns, shows a total length of 313 feet. Beyond a similar screen lies the big swimming bath, the *Natatio* (N). This is unroofed (the relatively thin surrounding walling indicates this) and flanked again by halls which may have afforded views, through colonnades, of aquatic games. To either side of the central axis lie the peristylar courts (P), apodyteria, and so on. Thick walls indicate vaulted rather than simple wooden roofs throughout.

Of particular interest to the plan-reader is the row of rooms on each side of the caldarium along the outside wall of the block. These rooms, which Simpson suggested rather attractively may have been for the use of poets and philosophers,[8] are shaped with reference to an interior emphasis.[9] This applies especially to the largest room of the line on each side. Basically oval this room is elaborated by niches to take up a shape unrelated to the neighbouring rooms or the external wall, an independence made clear only on plan.

The rest of the site, not included here, on which this building stands, maintaining absolutely the rule of symmetry (where one half is a mirror image of the other), is laid out with avenues of trees, and a stadium behind which are reservoirs serving the pipe system. Great exedrae, north-east and south-west, enclose chambers again shaped with no reference to this semicircular containing area. These are considered to have housed libraries. The whole stands on a levelled platform and returning partly around three walls, a double-storeyed arcade of shops and private baths.

So far we have merely described the arrangement of the plan in its relevance to the function of the building. But if we are to surmise on the architect's intention we require a special kind of scrutiny. The Thermae of Caracalla follow in a tradition which might have been established more than a hundred years before by the baths of Agrippa (20 B.C. added to by Hadrian and Severus), Titus (A.D. 79–81), and Trajan (A.D. 98–118), and was continued to the baths of Diocletian (A.D. 284–304). It is doubtful if there were any major differences between the latter of these in spite of the centuries spanned. It has been pointed out[10] that they were built as a sop to the people by the emperors, and as such were manifestly to gratify in terms of 'conspicuous waste' their sense of wonder and awe. Something of this sense of over-plus comes across from the very symmetry referred to above.

Mere symmetry in the disposition of a façade, or even a plan, can be achieved without a duplication of the accommodation. The main provisions of the Roman Bath: hot, warm, and cold baths, are supplied only once each, as they fall on the central axis, as does the stadium. Was it, one wonders, necessary, apart from the demands of visual balance, to have *two each* of everything else? And this duplication can only be bludgeoned into the consciousness of the

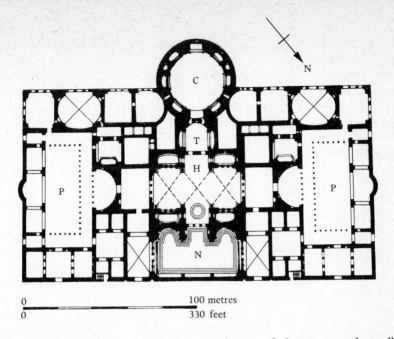

0	100 metres
0	330 feet

public visiting the baths by the long and perhaps confusing process of actually touring the site, wandering from hall to hall and from court to court, until a realization dawns that the almost endless reaches of these amenities is totally repeated on the other side of the building. Only on plan is the rigid schema so reduced that one is aware of it as a tidy and fairly simple pattern (just in view of the duplication): 313 feet from one end of the great central hall and its extensions to the other. Nearly one hundred metres. Clearly one is not going to cover that length very often in one visit to the baths. One is not going to *use* the vast extent of the building, but one is going to be aware of that vastness, the expense of equipping it, the incalculable man-hours implied in its fashioning, the scale beyond the individual client, or in fact all the clients for whom it was built, but not evidently beyond the emperor who so lavishly supplied it, nor, we may add with some complacency, the architect who conceived it. Alas, without the small scale required by his drawing board, he might not have been able to see it as a whole either. When we have the plan before us we soar over the mighty complex to find the architect wrought to the same scale as we are. Once the plans are handed to the builders, they take the scene over; the building slowly emerges in its gigantic proportions, perhaps overawing the architect himself, perhaps frightening the emperor into suppressing the architect's name and allowing only his own to be linked with the work. In any case the names of few architects have come down to us from Rome.

There is a point (after the general services and their zoning have been considered) where planning can become a game of pattern making, especially where roofing is a matter of covering rooms individually, as it evidently was here for the most part. All the generations influenced by the Romans enjoyed this to a certain extent, notably Palladio, and after him the Palladians and the English and other western architects of the later eighteenth century, though almost all of them were more restrained by roofing problems than were the Antonine Romans!

The Pantheon, Rome, 2nd century A.D.

We have indicated above (pp. 75ff.) that the Pantheon in Rome is a building evoking a strong emotional reaction in most of its visitors. How much of this emotional effect can be read in the plan depends partly on the observer's ability to read scale. The thickness of the walls and extent of the diameter will probably make him 'feel' a dome as the only feasible way to cover the whole interior, while the reduction of the bulk of the walls to achieve maximum supporting strength with a minimum of weight should, if he is alert, lead him to suppose the dome would carry a certain elasticity too. The oculus could perhaps not be deduced from the plan alone, except that no other form of light aperture is indicated.

For us to read in the plan the intention of its designer* it is essential first of all to free it in imagination from the clutter of building that has attached itself to the lower parts of the walls, and see it clearly as a circular plan with a rectangular portico. Then we must concentrate on the scale. Only with the realization that the walls are twenty feet thick at the base do we develop a proper respect for the dome carried by them, and an awareness of the implications of the impossibility of piercing them for windows. This is negative thinking, however, as false as to talk of 'walls' at all. There is in essence one wall, or vertical support for the dome which terminates in an aperture, perfectly adequate for light. Even the doorway is unemphasized and buried in such a way as to admit the merest ritual stream of light towards the main altar opposite. From the inside of the rotunda one can see almost the whole of the structure (only possible in a mono-spatial building) by being shown the deep burrowing into the lower part of the wall in contrast to the thin fabric at the rim of the oculus. This awareness is increased by the extra information given by the plan. Not only can we see clearly what inroads have been made into the thickness of the wall by the recesses visible from inside, but we see also between them

* It was built in the time of Hadrian and restored later under Septimius Severus and Caracalla. The name of the actual architect is not known.

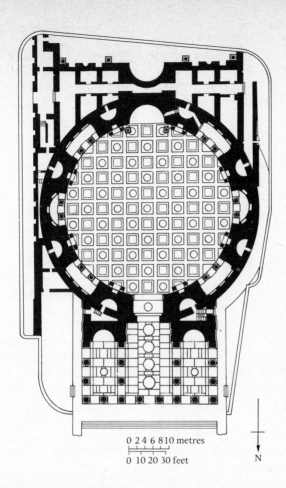

0 2 4 6 8 10 metres

0 10 20 30 feet

N

additional space cavities within the wall itself. We can therefore read that the actual structural parts of the wall form in essence a frame, or cage, presenting itself eventually as the lines of coffering in the dome. Externally none of this is visible, except a number of relieving arches in the brickwork, revealed when the walls were stripped of their facing.

The building is now sunk below street level, instead of being raised as it once was, and the plan shows how the much-criticized portico completely obscures the rotunda from the approach side. The great gaunt porch does seem over-stated when we see it on plan. It is thought to have been left over from an earlier building in this place, and presumably was too big to throw away.[11] A certain unhappiness in articulation seems to have been inevitable. What would have been an acceptable alternative? It is not for us to prescribe, but the rotunda carrying its dome is so advanced technically, the portico splendid but invoking the past in its trabeated front. Perhaps something smaller, simpler, based on the arch and vault system which now almost furtively supports its actual roof, would better prepare us for the interior.

Santa Sophia, Constantinople, 532–7

28 Santa Sophia was one of the earliest and certainly the most important of Byzantine churches. Although the principle of the pendentive was thoroughly understood by the time the great dome was raised, and in spite of the extreme finesse with which it was constructed, it suffered several times from earthquake damage and was eventually (in 1317) buttressed very heavily to strengthen the four colossal supporting piers.

The plan explains much to us that the sheer size of the building might cause us to miss. No plan can reproduce the often-described lightness and spatial fluidity of the dome series in this church: what it can, strangely, do, is remind us of the scale, which we lose in this serenely proportioned interior.

The atrium usually shown on the plan is no longer there, and does not seem (any more than the equally outdated portico of the Pantheon) to have been very powerfully integrated with the rest of the structure, which is not reached until arrival at the inner narthex introduces the visitor to a position where, through a

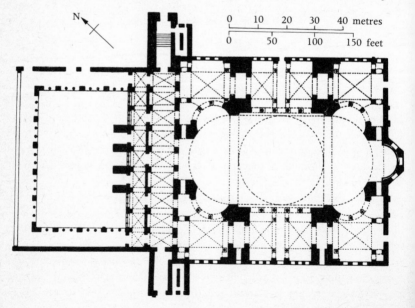

frame of limited enclosure, the vast spaces of the interior may partly be seen. Under the first half-dome of the series this becomes a full reality, and from the plan we can see how the architect lifted his three domes like mounting bubbles on to the piers that space out the whole project. Vast galleries (but reaching only half way to the springing of the central dome) crowd around the huge volume of the central space. Here on the plan we can see how the simple but enormous structural system depends upon the great piers, the walls reduced for perhaps the first time on this scale merely to screens. We can also see how the piers themselves are pierced to form side aisles. The effect of the upper structure is prophesied by the plan, which shows the distribution of weight on the opened-up piers, and reports upon the light spaciousness achieved by open exedrae, galleries, and the non-supporting screen walls full of window openings. The plans are furthermore quite enough to demonstrate the unique sophistication of Santa Sophia among Byzantine churches, in this sense happily named!

Cathedral of Notre Dame, Amiens, begun 1220

The reduction in the continuity of load-bearing walls formed the great contribution of the late twelfth century. This was accompanied by a necessary struggle to increase the flexibility of the vaulting system. The West started with none of the sophisticated engineering skill that had been developed by the Romans. All that they had known and evolved was lost with the overthrow of Rome, and the barbarians had to start from scratch. A thousand years of technology could not again produce anything of the magnitude of Santa Sophia, but something was achieved, certainly in artistry, perhaps too in engineering, though it was to prove a dead end. The extent of structural achievement at Amiens was a nave of 40 less than forty feet wide. The Basilica of Constantine was more than twice as wide, if not quite so high, in uninterrupted space. The Romans had pushed ahead with the more contemporary and flexible materials of brick and concrete, available everywhere, easily produced on the site, equally appropriate for civil and domestic buildings. The builders of the Middle Ages attended only to the temple, using for it the somewhat anachronistic material of stone, with which they wrought the splendid, esoteric and impractical filigree of their aspiring forms. Impractical, because it did not introduce any type valid to architecture or architectural structure generally; it threw up half a hundred great churches, inward-looking towards their own perfecting, and thus, although we recognize a type, it was a type containing the germs of its own decay. Amiens is the first maturity, and after Amiens, virtually, there is nothing.

Something of this sickness, something of the hysterical balance achieved surely pulsates with the delicacy of a butterfly's wing over a plan of Amiens,

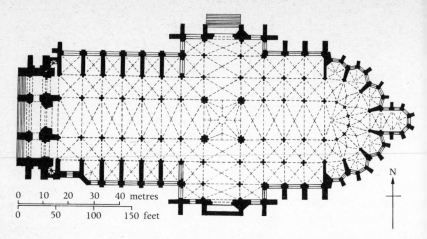

0 10 20 30 40 metres
0 50 100 150 feet

N

which is as much a plan of the vaulting as of the floor bays. One does not read in the plan, except by a great effort of concentration, what one sees in person within or outside the cathedral. There one is aware of darkness and light, of the imminence of stone, of the great carved mouldings even if only of the pier bases. Outside it is the tall piers, the sweeping buttresses, the curiously exclud-ing quality of Gothic glass from the outside, gargoyle and crocket and steep roof, or, on the west façade, only the west façade: deeply recessed triple doors, massive piers, endless carving. This is all gauged to the human eye, the human scale. Nothing of it is obvious on plan. Instead we are confronted with the ridiculously reduced version—only comprehensible as a whole because of this reduction—of the total cathedral. But much is elucidated in this intellectual statement. We can see why at the west end only the façade is visible: because the block of towers and portals is not a part of the structural system as such, but precedes and blocks at the same time, as effectively as do the pylons of the Egyptian temple. Once through the portals, however, one is caught up in the tight mesh of the system. High nave lifted aloft by nave arcade, pressed at the sides by vaults and buttresses, tied finally by flying buttress linking wall to pier. Which way is the pressure concentrated? Are the walls kept from falling out or falling in? This is not clear, but it all looks efficient and logical and no doubt is left in our minds that every member is present and in its intended place.

The scholastic background of the builders of the cathedrals has been some-what emphasized in interpreting their quality. Even the ultimate development of rib out of plate tracery has been seen as a means of continuity, through the glass, of internal and external space symbolizing the fusion of intellect and spirit.*

* But see above p. 87.

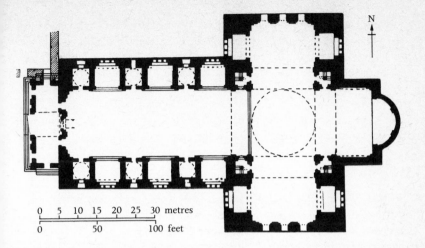

N

Sant'Andrea, Mantua, begun 1472

When we move in imagination from the nave of Amiens to that of a Renaissance church like Sant'Andrea, first we find a very much wider span, and second it is as though all columnar supports have been cleared away. The explanation for this is immediately evident if we turn to the plan of the later church. The nave is 60 feet wide, covered by a continuous barrel vault interrupted only by the dome on pendentives at the crossing. There are no side aisles, but chapels line the walls of nave and transepts, and the crosswalls of these no doubt ingeniously provide the buttressing necessary to take the thrust of the vault so that there is a minimum of masonry support, fully manifested only at the corners of nave and transepts. That is all: simple, contemporary, efficient. The impression is of a calculated sturdiness rather than the excessive bulk of some Byzantine domed and vaulted churches, though the same material, brick, is used here. It may well be the use of brick (of which Alberti approved as a building material) that led to the suppression of columns, free or attached, in this church and the use only of flat pilasters. All the rest of the designer's effort was concentrated in scaling his elevations inside and out to form those relations between parts that would please his neo-platonist audience. The plan shows that, sturdy though the sections are, the loads are reasonably distributed and elastically supported. The fifteenth century did not have all the structural resources of the Romans, but they were moving towards a time when they would recognize the implications when they saw them.

Only from the plan can we read the actual relations of the famous porch to the church itself. Presumably the west front could have been treated like the

transepts: themselves pedimented portals, as we may still see by the now somewhat battered form of the north entrance. But Alberti evidently wanted something more subtly affirmative and used (both in plan and elevation) the propor-
tionate relation in void and solid of the nave sides. We can see on plan, and may
confirm on elevation, the large central opening flanked by the two smaller ones.
It is indeed puzzling in confrontation of the church to see what part the porch
plays in the whole: only the recognition of the deliberate adding of a feature,
echoing the interior ordinance reveals the architect's thinking.

The Château of Chambord, begun 1519

The idea of symmetry tends to be associated with the classical rather than the
medieval, and yet if we pause to think about it we shall see that it is properly
associated with all structure and certainly all formal structure. Whether we are
influenced by living creatures like ourselves which, externally at least, have
forms consisting of two echoing halves about a central line, or whether empir-
ical discovery that the most direct form of balance in a structure is to pit one
equivalent against another, man's great structural works tend to have been for
the most part symmetrical. A hut will turn out symmetrical because it is easier
to make that way, but when the builder wants to increase his accommodation
and make it consist of two or three cells instead of one, it is not always necessary
that these be the same size, or a repetition of each other, and they are not
necessarily symmetrically disposed. Most small housing units, whether in a so-
called 'classical' or 'non-classical' community or era, simply make no reference
to symmetry in external appearance, though in certain elements, like peristyles
or halls, structural logic may produce a symmetrical unit. In fact this structural
logic will produce symmetry more often than not, symmetry being less an
aesthetic requirement than the result of physical balance.

Even when it is evoked deliberately and written, as it were, into the plan,
it may very well not be for reasons of aesthetic. Most military structures,
fortifications notably, are strongly symmetrical in order to reproduce
formally adequate defence points. Moreover a circular shape for the plan of a
defence tower is logical, to give as nearly as possible an outlook through 360°.
Near to this comes the polygon. It is easier to reinforce an angle than a flat or
curved wall.

The Château of Chambord was not built for defence, though it is not inconceivable that a stout or even defensive appearance may have been considered
appropriate by François I for his hunting box so deeply set in the countryside.
The double-bastion system with the royal residence set like a keep within the
protective walls of the Cour d'Honneur, is admirably designed, both for the

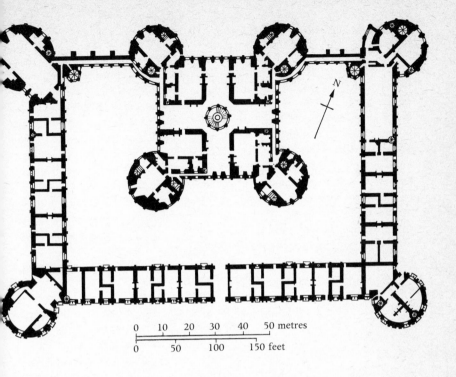

continuous view of the huntsmen during the day from the roofs so easily frequented by the ladies and others who were not hunting, and for the reception of the riders when they finally returned to headquarters. It is at once apparent in looking at the plan, that these battlement towers are not any longer required for an old protective rôle, since they are vast enough to contain within their cylindrical walls, grand chambers of rectangular and other shapes.

The 'keep' is the Château itself, and within the playful rigour of its square four-towered form it allows for a symmetry of another more sophisticated kind. The floor is in fact cut by a vast cruciform hall into a 'cross-in-square' arrangement of which the central feature is the famous double-flight circular staircase, where two independent helices pursue each other to the upper floor. No concession is made at all to the cylindrical shape of the towers, so that one finds throughout the 'cave and crystal' relationship. Only on such a colossal scale would this extravagant treatment have been conceivable, and only in the plan is this giant whimsicality revealed, reminding us of the Italian Mannerism that so strongly influenced the art of François's court.

San Carlo alle Quattro Fontane, Rome, 1638

8 San Carlino (without its cloister and adjacent conventual buildings) might easily have been set in one of the cylindrical towers of Chambord, even with (as Sir Banister Fletcher might have said) much waste of space, though in fact in its own irregular and equally 'buried' site no space has been wasted at all. Like the lower rooms at Chambord the shape of the church has been designed without reference to the shape of the available space but making as much use as possible of its extension, especially in length. The nave does not run ideally east–west but on a compromise axis fitting in with the long axis of the site, that is roughly north-west/south-east, the altar of course at the south-east end.

This is the kind of design whose intentions become intellectually clear only upon scrutiny of the plan. It was not Borromini's first design that was built, though evidently some sort of diamond shape was always intended. This is formed on plan by four concavities linked by four convexities which form the well-known undulations of the walls. Both concave and convex sections of wall are treated with meticulous symmetry, though doors in the convex portions of the walls lead out to four quite differently shaped and sized spaces outside the nave itself. This is only apparent on the plan, where in two cases 'buried' chapels are given their own small symmetries, and every scrap of possible space has been used without referring to the shape of the boundary walls.

Two of these form an awkward street corner, flattened across the angle to accommodate one of the four fountains which give their name to the street. The narrow surface of wall left to form the 'west front' of the church was completed after Borromini's death, but is so perfectly a continuation of the attitude producing the internal designing that we are left without any doubt that it proceeded from his own intentions. The wall surface, if one can call it that, is shaped without any overt reference to, or link with, the interior, but relates to it in the employment of an alternately convex and concave treatment. It has been pointed out that the central feature of this façade bears a strong resemblance to that of the rock temple/tomb of El Khasne at Petra, and in fact the whole façade is to a certain extent a sophisticated version of it. Why the façade of a rock-cut tomb should have been chosen as the basis for the façade of this 'excavated' Baroque church remains an unanswered but fascinating question. Surely Borromini himself must have recognized his own allusion?

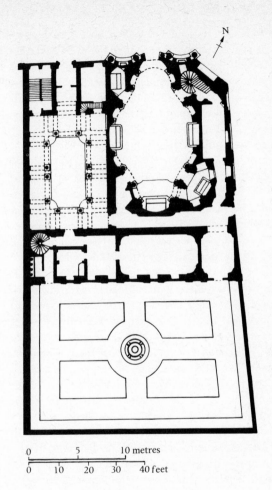

N

0   5   10 metres

0 10 20 30 40 feet

St. Stephen Walbrook, London, 1672

The plans of Wren's City churches look at once prosaic and insubstantial. It may be that being accustomed, as we are, to the plans of medieval churches, we are also used to the chunky silhouette formed by stone walls, and even where, as often in Italy, later churches are built of brick, they are usually designed to carry vaults or domes and thus are not always immediately distinguishable in plan from stone structures. Apart from the stone used for coigns and other trim, and presumably a certain amount of rubble of which many of the old churches in the City had been built, Wren's materials had been brick, tile, timber, and plaster, and of these he had made competent use. His sites, as everyone knows, were confined and often irregular: the combining of parishes during the re-building after the fire had meant larger congregations, the vast area of rebuilding meant a rapid absorption of men and materials. He was committed to build quickly, cheaply, and commodiously: it is also emphasized that he was building virtually without precedent for a Protestant congregation for whom traditional churches were by function and association undesirable.

All this can be read in the plan of St. Stephen Walbrook, built about 1676, the time of the accepting of the Warrant Design for St. Paul's. Here the site was not so irregular as to affect the simple rectangle of the plan, which is sur-rounded by a regular system of windows, unevenly spaced but symmetrical about the long axes, and providing a subsidiary 'axis' across the diameter of the dome. The plan of course cannot convey that these windows are elliptical and set very high in the walls, just below what may be called the 'clear-story' windows, though there is in actuality no roof for them to 'clear'. What we bring to our reading of the plan is our knowledge that Wren's windows are generally for lighting and not for views, which here are unavailable.

Looking then at this spare and baggy-looking plan with its dome set out by a ring of eight slender columns, we feel its dry lightness. It obviously exerts no more weight or thrust than the flat or vaulted canopies carried on the remaining eight columns, completing the rectangle of support, and affirming the wood-and-plaster construction of Wren's vaulting system. Stone presses down, visually as well as actually, displacing considerable volumes for its supporting bases. Brick and timber often appear to be leaping upward, hardly encroaching on the spaces they define or penetrate. This is the character of the City churches. Emphasizing the simple box-like rectangle (for the canopies do not anywhere cancel this) is the absence on plan of a projecting chancel or apse. This is defined quite adequately (and even perhaps brilliantly) by its setting in one of the arches that carry the pendentives of the dome. The altar is not excluded, but reduced in accordance with Protestant propriety. John

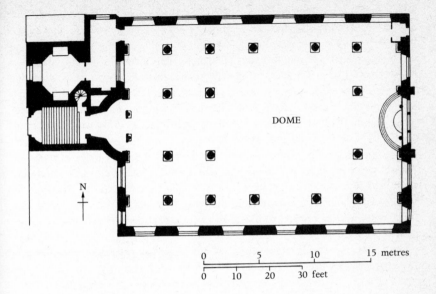

DOME

N

| 0 | 5 | 10 | 15 metres |

| 0 | 10 | 20 | 30 feet |

Summerson points out that the same technique is used to 'provide' transepts.[12]

Finally the west end offers a characteristic piece of Wren's planning. A steep stair is necessary to lift us from street level, and this, almost totally enclosed, delivers us into a vestibule from which we are generously funnelled into the nave. The defining walls here are thick, with the character of excavation, and contiguous with those of the tower base, providing in the thickness a spiral stair. All of Wren's towers are substantial in construction, and the indication of heavy supporting walls is again characteristic. From the plan we cannot see, but we can understand, what is often the only part now visible of these churches, the square sturdy tower, with its delicate sophisticated steeple.

17

Lord Derby's, Grosvenor Square, London, 1773–4 (demolished 1862)

To read the plan of a Robert Adam town house is to make a journey through it, a visual delight not unlike that of penetrating the shallows and depths of a de Hoogh interior. It lies, as we see at once, between two long 'party' walls characteristic of a London town plot, and we begin by crossing the well communicating with the basement by steps leading up to the porch. Inside we find ourselves in a large entrance hall, its basically rectangular shape modulated by cupboards and niches in the walls. To our left is a fireplace, straight ahead is a door leading to the stair well, should we wish to mount, lit amply no doubt by a roof light at the top of the well; on the farther side is a door to the dining room. We are more likely, however, to have been attracted to a formally set door on the right of the entrance hall, opposite the fire, which leads by way of a sort of indoor portico to the Ante-Room, where, as visitors, we are halted before proceeding to the parlour. This ante-room turns its back on the street, which it seems now to reject, denying its proximity by means of a curved wall which tends to prepare us for the movement into the parlour. Again we have a sort of portico, between whose columns we pass into the parlour itself. This is a large room, with a fireplace flanked by niches in the long outer wall (which is thereby not associated in our minds with the exterior) and a door to a service stair in the other wall. At its end are windows to the court outside which leads to the stables, and another way into the Great Eating Room.

Once here, we are in a large room whose shape has been determined by its own character. Its plan has become a great long-sided oval, with curved walls at both ends, surrounded by niches and doors to cupboards, a big fireplace on one side and windows to the court on the other. At the far end is a door to the library, again an oval with its axis at right angles to that of the dining room, whose curved sides make a continuation of the theme proposed by the ante-room near the entrance hall and followed by the dining room. Behind the library are a dressing room, and service rooms and staircase.

This urbane version of 'excavation' architecture (alas now demolished) is characteristic of Robert Adam's town houses, where the ingenious arrangements of rooms between the long inflexible party walls may be seen again and again, the visitor led into the narrow depths through a beguiling series of rooms *en suite* and just sufficiently modified from the simple rectangle to throw the interest inward from any speculation about the limits or limitations of the site. The extreme polish and adequacy of the internal arrangements would render quite superfluous anything beyond a conformity in the disposition of the usual polite three-storeyed façade.

The reader is afforded a sort of gratification, as though some of the architect's ingenuity is to his credit; and in fact the appreciation of ingenuity always involves some share in it. This is certainly one of the pleasures of reading and comprehending a plan, that the reader shares for a moment the architect's approach to his building.

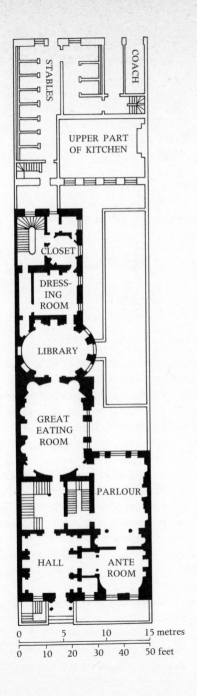

STABLES

COACH

UPPER PART
OF KITCHEN

CLOSET

DRESS-
ING
ROOM

LIBRARY

GREAT
EATING
ROOM

PARLOUR

HALL

ANTE
ROOM

0   5   10   15 metres

0   10   20   30   40   50 feet

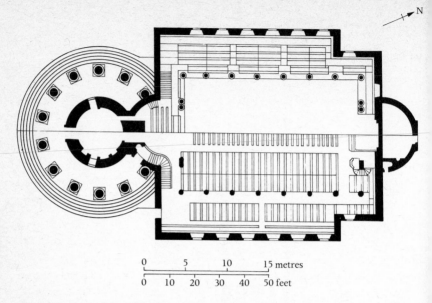

```
0          5          10          15 metres
0    10    20    30    40    50 feet
```

All Souls Langham Place, London, 1822

Langham Place, half way up Nash's 'Royal Mile' between Carlton House and
Regent's Park, has little about it now to remind us of the great Regency
entrepreneur, except All Souls Church, still one of the most graceful things in
London. But if we want to forget the lumpish buildings which now surround
the junction between upper Regent Street and Portland Place we must look at
the plan, which still preserves the original shape and reminds us of the brilliant
flair behind the project as a whole.

The Church Commissioners were one of the bodies whose patronage made
possible the establishment of this oddly successful route: Nash evidently engin-
eered their purchase of a site on a particular bend of the road and designed All
Souls especially for it, and a very pretty piece of ingenuity it is. Nash seems to
have had a gift for putting his finger on the sensitive spot, and so inevitably did
this gesture emerge that few ordinary Londoners seem to notice it, except to
realize that it completes a vista in a city where vistas are not infrequently
accidents or afterthoughts.

The church itself is merely an ample box of the Wren genre, unremarkable
externally and probably seen infrequently internally except by its own congregation and amateurs of architecture. (If it were not so close to the B.B.C.
building, and therefore a useful landmark, it would be probably even less
noticed.) The brilliant part of it is, of course, the vestibule, almost a total circle

and therefore unhappily related (on plan anyway) with the box. This kind of insensitivity was perhaps characteristic of Nash, but it would be worse than a quibble to insist upon it here, since it has produced such a clever, if disingenuous handling of what might have been a disastrous situation in the buckling of the street at that place. Indeed Langham Place is only saved now from being a worse disaster by the brittle presence of this church, towards which, at least, the bruised eye can still gratefully turn.

The brilliance of the circular vestibule arises from the fact that wherever one stands in Langham Place, wherever one has come from, or wherever one catches any glimpse of it at all, the cylindrical design appears fully stated, and since one cannot from anywhere see the 'body' of the church very clearly, self-effacing as it is, it is as though one always saw the vestibule from its main aspect. The peristyle of tall ionic columns (with all capitals designed to make an angular impact) contains a small internal cylinder, the vestibule itself, rising above the peristyle to become a plinth for a second peristyle surrounding the drum supporting, in its turn, the spire. This latter (and in fact the whole vestibule) has an unusual *insouciance*, a sense of brave sufficiency. The cylindrical surfaces of columns and enclosing walls catch every possible shaft of light and insist on a range of shadow, so that it is never totally grey or dull.

All this is not discernible on the plan itself. But the plan explains everything that might puzzle the visitor. Or rather it explains why the visitor is not puzzled or curious, or experiences anything but a passing amused delight as he goes up (or down) between the Crescent and the Circus.

Villa Savoye at Poissy, 1928–30

If we look at the plan of the '*étage d'habitation*' (which is to say the *piano nobile*) of the Villa Savoye we shall see at once as regular a structural layout as at the Queen's House or any other classical building. This time the system is formed [19] by a grid of supports carrying the layers of reinforced concrete floor. Themselves fairly regularly disposed, they carry a wall-less structure, strictly rectangular on plan, seemingly less so on elevation because of *terrasses*, cut backs, ramps, and so forth which link the levels.

Here is an early example (1928–30) of Le Corbusier's free plan. In three dimensions a pleasing informality offers us the choice of ramp or stair to approach the house from the ground below it. Once on the *étage d'habitation* we move easily from room to hall to *terrasse*, now offered an uninhibited vista through long unbroken windows, now finding ourselves in neatly appointed kitchen or *cabinet de toilette*.

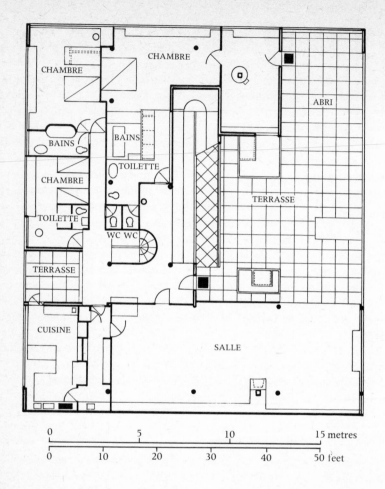

CHAMBRE

CHAMBRE

ABRI

BAINS

BAINS

TOILETTE

CHAMBRE

TERRASSE

TOILETTE

WC WC

TERRASSE

CUISINE

SALLE

0		5		10		15 metres
0	10	20	30	40		50 feet

But from the plan we first read the structural system: the ground floor has been merely an approach to the house proper, and a support for it; the living floor is shown here with the sturdy system of supports continuing to rise to the roof level, and the delicate system of light walls zoning off the areas of activity, not forming repetitive boxes but precisely defining the scope, encircling a bath here, a closet or stair there. Some of the resultant shapes are surprising, unusual, often stimulating. Perhaps most surprisingly many areas take up a basically rectangular shape. But perhaps after all this is not surprising: rectilinearity is either geometrically normal or parallel to our own bipedal and visual activities. It is more natural to us than we always remember.

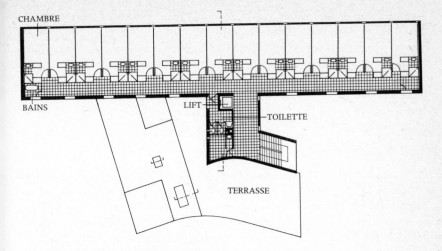

CHAMBRE

BAINS   LIFT

—TOILETTE

TERRASSE

The Swiss Pavilion in Paris, 1930

The rectangular unit becomes obligatory in any building which is multi-storeyed because it must repeat its services, not only on every floor, but many times on each floor. The multi-cellular building becomes almost inevitably the egg-box. Le Corbusier worked on the reasonable assumption that when a type of accommodation suitable for one of the occupants had been worked out, that precise accommodation should be repeated, since if it were not, what was put in its place must be worse or better. That is not to say of course that an architect may not provide different sets of accommodation, two and three roomed flats for example. The Swiss Pavilion at the Cité Universitaire in Paris is a fairly straight-forward example, since it is a block of single rooms all for the same type of tenant, the student. The problem was therefore to design a suitable unit, repeat it along each floor over a number of floors, and to add some communal rooms.

    The plan is very easy to read. A typical floor shows that once a good aspect is chosen this is maintained for all rooms. They face over the extended grounds of the site. The egg-box presents its open wall-less side to this, and a thin line shows that glass covers the whole façade. A long passage on each floor gives access to the rooms. This would be as long as (but no longer than) is comfortable. To make this possible, vertical access occurs as near the centre of the corridor as possible; here too toilet services are located. These appear somewhat meagre to our eyes, but were undoubtedly in accordance with French hostel standards of 1930!

    It will be seen that by using his favourite system of the block on *pilotis* the

20

architect renders the amenities of the lowest floor of rooms precisely the same as those of the other floors. He uses the ground floor for the entrance and general rooms which include a library. Here, because he does not have to fit rooms into a repeating system, he introduces that lyrical curved wall which has given distinction to the building as a whole and rendered it unique. There is no reason for it except visual and tactile excitement, qualities which distinguish the work of art.

The 1931 Exhibition House at Berlin

21   It is generally agreed that Ludwig Mies van der Rohe was the Purist exponent-in-chief of the 'free plan'. Nowhere is this better demonstrated than in this design for a house which, built for an exhibition, was therefore uninhibited either by the cross-currents emanating from a client or by the exigencies of a specific site. One might expect then the complete statement of the architect's personal aesthetic and structural preference. Two things are immediately observable in looking at the plan, which are in fact characteristic of this architect's mode of designing: one is the use of a single storey, thus promoting structural simplicity, and the other, emerging from this, is the use of walls almost solely as screens dividing the ground area with a minimum of angles and breaks, each 'sheet' of wall or glass remaining as whole or 'pure' as possible. Walls continue their screening or defining function even when no longer protected by roofs and thus are seen on plan as vertical and horizontal lines dividing up the area into zones of suggested but not enforced activity. Total closure is found only in zones for which privacy or protection is essential: the kitchen (C), the bath, the WC (A, B). For the rest, space is as continuously flowing as human movement from one activity to another. Indeed the ambience can hardly be said to change: one sleeps, eats, listens to music, or loafs on the terrace in the same fluid element.

The design is the exposition of a principle and not the solution to a specific problem. It can therefore exhibit a purity unusual in an actual domestic work. Space—as indicated by the furniture included in the plan—is generously provided: only the kitchen quarters are economically scaled. A mesh of delicate verticals supports the flat roofs. Walls terminate zones rather than the structure. Thus a length of wall provides privacy and direction to the dining area. Another gives a background for conversation. The enclosure of the bathroom gives a subdivision to the bedroom area, which is kept intact by continuous glass and a vast (but protected) terrace. Everywhere is the subtlety of closer and further vertical planes overlapping each other with suggestive reference to attainable space beyond.

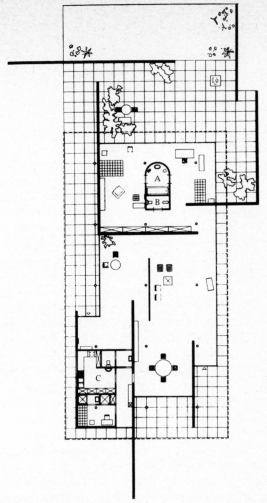

It is interesting to compare this pavilion with the well-known and almost contemporary (1930) Tugendhat house by the same architect. This is, as one might expect, a little (but not much) more closely zoned, with not quite such a sense of unlimited areas of continuous wall defining. It has however the same quality of discriminating and fastidious disposition: screened dining area, lightly divided living zones. The same minimal supports carry a flat roof, which this time supports terraces and an upper storey of bedrooms—three large groups of them in fact. The spaces within the structural demarcation are in the same scale of generosity as in the less specific exhibition-house scheme.

Conclusion

Play Sculpture and Play-pen

It is supposed in any consideration of planned environment that planning waits upon functional requirements, as structure waits upon planning. It must be realized though, that if the planners are imaginative creators, with, as the best of them have, an urgent and selective vision, environmental design will at least partly, and perhaps largely, determine its own function. Certain things must happen in certain environments: certain things cannot happen in them. When Le Corbusier was first introduced to the Chandigarh site he seems to have been obsessed with the cattle—white and grey—which stood about on the land. They, and the nervous silhouette of the peripheral hills were among the first things he drew, together with what looks like an antique aqueduct. The arches were retained in the sophisticated entrance loggia to the Assembly: photographs do not reveal whether the oxen have any place on the suave and severely discriminatory vehicle approaches, but they appear, vestigially, in mural reliefs. The nearer an architect approaches to being a great artist, the nearer he approaches to being a ruthless autocrat. Only his brilliance renders that autocracy tolerable, and the variation possible among members of his profession. Little as the imaginative visions of great men coincide, or even harmonize, we could not support any single manner infinitely. Though they may be among the greatest works of their kind, we could not sit for a lifetime looking at Michelangelo's Last Judgement and listening to the St. Matthew Passion.

This dominance of the Great Artist becomes sometimes formidable in architecture, when we must find great brilliance and meaning and inexhaustible stimulation or refreshment in forms that have to be perpetually confronted and known in the daily course of living. Civic centre and public place, office block, school and university, research laboratory and association building; every place in which we spend our time and work as individuals is provided for us by the taste and decision of bodies unapproachable by us, and perhaps wholly uncongenial to us. Who can tolerate the work of all artists? We can turn our backs on those we do not wish to regard, but who can turn his back on his own office desk, or the board room across whose massy tables he daily confronts his colleagues? Happy we are who have made, or had some share in making, our own immediate environment. As for living in a great work of art, some of us might prefer to settle for less, and yet, as has been suggested earlier, if we cannot live with what is designed for that purpose, is it a successful design? Well, yes, it might be—for others than ourselves. A dwelling is not always—is not usually—(perhaps never should be) tailored to an individual, though it be, we hope, purpose made. A work of art may or may not be a commission; even if it is, it tends today not to be designed for, or even designated for, a specific person, though persons are envisaged in relation to its ultimate function, and it is with this in mind that the term 'play-sculpture' has been invoked here.

The growth of the idea that sculptural arrangements might be invaded by spectators, and—because of the scrambling and climbing often involved—particularly by children, might have its origins in the audience-participation that was first introduced into Dada performances (and usually attended in these instances with real aggression and resentment on the part of the participants). Environmental art provides a considerable measure of audience participation, and we are familiar today with the many examples of constructions of kinetic and other mobility which require the collaboration of the spectator to set them 'working'.

'Play' sculpture is only one variety among art works which invite this collaboration, and its literal intention is shown by its being set up in parks and playgrounds where children can use it as apparatus. It is questionable whether any aesthetic service is thus provided for the children themselves, but there is no doubt that great pleasure is afforded the onlookers, many of whom feel that this is a way of putting abstract art to some use and therefore justifying its existence.

The intention of this kind of sculpture is sometimes equivocal, because it may not have been actually made for children to play on, though the sculptor does not (or says he does not) mind their doing so. This would suggest that it is considered by the artist equally valid and meaningful whether the human participant is present or not.

This situation is surely paralleled in some architectural situations. There is a sculptural quality about the building which can provide its own visual fulfilment, and there is a tendency, when people are present, for them to explore and experience the building itself rather than to use it as a setting. Monumental temples and shrines provide examples from antiquity; perhaps one could find many instances in the orient where a certain animation colours the building more than it does in the West. One thinks of large Buddhas forming temples, or perhaps those sphinxes and man-headed lions that made approach avenues to Egyptian temples. Caryatid porches in Greece offer an equivocal situation, as architectural environment with 'presence' more than the human solely. Intricate arrangement, which means arrangement for a visual effect rather than utility, provides something of this quality, and with reference to what we have considered earlier, must be regarded as the equivalent to a sculptural surround.

Traditional sculpture tends to be of stone or clay or other moulded material, and we still speak of 'sculptural' forms as those which have weightiness or plastic modelling about them. In this context we could offer certain buildings of Gaudi's as 'sculptural', his church in Barcelona, his plastic and non-formal flats, and his fantasies in the Guell Park. Le Corbusier's Ronchamp chapel is often referred to as sculptural, and we have already quoted the Greek temple generally, perhaps with particular reference to the Parthenon, as being regarded as a work of 'sculpture', though here of course the carved forms are of that precision which is essentially classical. A structure which provided much interest in the thirties was Lubetkin's Penguin Pool at the London Zoo, with its playful arrangement of ramps up which the engaging little creatures could waddle. A similar activity is prepared for humans in the Guggenheim Museum —and in all museums where movement past the exhibition is controlled. Designing for controlled movement of this sort is seen most simply demonstrated in the ramps and flyovers of modern motorways. 'Play-sculpture' treatment seems most appropriate in public buildings where movement-direction is not implicit, but where a measure of restlessness and impermanence is dominant. I am thinking here perhaps of such places as the public halls of post-offices and banks, or public information centres, galleries, and arcades that form pedestrian throughways and casual meeting places. These are all appropriate places for sculptural architecture or sculptures themselves. Whether the public pauses, waits, or moves on, the visual environment can be a conscious part of their experience. Stimulating or arresting forms and vistas may happily participate in settings that are meant for the spectator whose presence is temporary, because they are then part of a moving experience to be shortly exchanged for other visual experiences. This may apply even to hotels and other places of temporary sojourn.

The extent to which dwelling places intended to offer permanent residence should reflect this 'sculptural' character varies so considerably with the occupant that it seems at once unsuitable for any but separately sited houses. A block of dwellings would clearly be more viable if it is to some extent general in aesthetic statement, at least in planning and internal control. By this is not meant that any compromise in design quality is desirable, but merely that handling that promotes any violent visual stimulus may be difficult to 'sell' to a number of clients of differing temperament. The private house needs only the co-operation of one tenant with his architect, and may therefore be a far more unequivocal statement. All that need be said here is that, if 'play-sculpture' is to be provided, the architect has to establish a thoroughly tried *rapprochement* with the client, who must not be the child of the 'play-pen' proclivities.

Whatever range of classifications may be propounded for buildings, there is a kind of shelter in extensive demand in which the activities carried on also prohibit any great degree of architectural detail designing. Reference is here intended to such functions as those of factories of many kinds, but more particularly workshops, studios, and spaces for a multitude of fabrications whose equipment does not call for that degree of architectural finesse in arrangement and especially finish with which we normally associate it. The analogy of the play-pen has been chosen, because the play-pen provides little more than a defined (and thus limited) place where the child can assemble his own desired equipment and provide for his own small industries, whether these be with paints, bricks, counters, or any other articles contributary to his business.

It is not of course suggested here that artisans or artists, whether professional or amateur, should work in a shambles, or be housed with their tools and work surfaces in a manner or in structures inadequately designed or visually unappealing. The important quality is flexibility, adaptability, an unobtrusive behaviour of container surfaces and limiting walls, a lack of encroachment either in actual substance or in visual insistence, a reticence in fact and lack of aggressive demand. However the container may express itself and even strut or prance externally, internally it is the things contained that are of importance, and the person or persons manipulating those things, who may well desire enlargement of the space available as those things take shape or are dismantled (as in the case of vehicle repair or assemblage). Visual meaning here can only arise from the logical and known relations of the objects and fragments of objects normally housed, in the sense of spatial adequacy and undemanding surface treatment: oil on the floor of a workshop, sawdust in a carpenter's shop, paint in a studio, or muck in a stable, are norms to be designed for. Since the Crystal Palace provided its graceful and totally appropriate accommodation for the unrelated odds and ends of the Great Exhibition, the aviary-type building has been re-invoked many times for the housing of miscellany. Not usually in the past the most distinguished buildings in the environment, they have recently received the same exciting treatment accorded to such structures as sports and other congregational pavilions. Certainly Nervi's factories are very distinguished indeed, and the emphasis we have noted above on the provision of cover with maximum span augurs well for the development of a more imaginative attitude to the erection of these often very vast shelters. Frei Otto's design for the roofing of a harbour in Bremen is one of many indications of spanning possibilities. Even in unusual situations one finds the experiment of planning with a minimum of rigid screens. The Architecture School of IIT in Chicago, Crown Hall, by Mies van der Rohe, is described by Reyner Banham. 'Effectively,' writes Banham, 'it is a single room, big enough to contain the entire school, and free of columns because the structure is carried in giant trusses clear over the roof, which is hung from them.'[1] Here is the play-pen *par excellence*. Its special function allows it to be what Banham calls 'a crystal casket of meditative calm'.

The need for this kind of designing is not confined to large industry. A domestic setting has often to cater for similar activities on a smaller scale. Cooking, sewing, carpentry, garden cultivation all require space allocation regarded as normal but not always adequately provided for. How often is the domestic allocation really shaped for the housing of buckets, bicycles, and garden gloves; for the setting up of electric railway circuits, ham radios, homing pigeons, dog and cat breeding, and do it yourself projects of all kinds? But even all this is not our major concern here. The larger issue to be faced is whether our domestic designing caters sufficiently for *homo fabricans* or even *facens*, which each of us, at least sometimes, is. Our times become less spacious, we know, and we must suppose that we shrink to fit them. A recently discussed interest in 'multi-purpose' designing offers a ray of hope for one way out of some of the encroaching deprivations. Buildings or even rooms adaptable to various functions at least promote the hope of various functions.

Select Bibliography

I   Selection from list of books consulted:

Theory and History of Architecture

Collingwood, R. G., *The Principles of Art*, The Clarendon Press, Oxford, 1938

Collins, Peter, *Changing Ideals in Modern Architecture 1750–1950*, Faber and Faber, London, 1971

Graham, J. W., *The Palaces of Crete*, Princeton University Press, 1962

Martienssen, Heather, *The South African Architectural Record*, August 1950, pp. 176–82, The Nature of Baroque: One: The Architecture of Excavation

Martienssen, Rex, *The Idea of Space in Greek Architecture*, Witwatersrand University Press, Johannesburg, 1956

Michelis, P. A., *An Aesthetic Approach to Byzantine Art*, Batsford, London, 1955

Nervi, Pier Luigi, *Aesthetics and Technology in Building*, trans. Robert Einaudi, Harvard University Press and Oxford University Press, 1966

Panofsky, Erwin, *Gothic Architecture and Scholasticism*, Meridian Books, New York, 1960

Rasmussen, Steen Eiler, *Experiencing Architecture*, Chapman and Hall, London, 1959

Rudofsky, Bernard, *Architecture without Architects*, Museum of Modern Art, New York, 1965

Venturi, Robert, *Complexity and Contradiction in Architecture*, Museum of Modern Art, New York, 1966

Zevi, Bruno, *Architecture as Space*, trans. Milton Grendel, Horizon Press, New York, 1957

Contemporary Architecture

Banham, Reyner, *Guide to Modern Architecture*, The Architectural Press, London, 1962

—*Theory and Design in the First Machine Age*, The Architectural Press, London, 1962

Besset, Maurice, *Who was Le Corbusier?*, Skira, Geneva, 1968

Boesiger, W., and Girsberger, H., *Le Corbusier 1910–1965*, Thames and Hudson, London, 1967

Conrads, Ulrich, ed., *Programmes and manifestos on 20th century architecture*, Lund Humphries, London, 1970

Hatje, Gerd, ed., *Encyclopaedia of Modern Architecture*, Thames and Hudson, London, 1963

Heyer, Paul, *Architects on Architecture: New Directions in America*, Walker and Company, New York, 1966

Hitchcock, H-R., and Johnson, Philip, *The International Style*, Norton and Co. Ltd., New York, 1966

Jaffé, Hans L. C., *De Stijl 1917–1931*, Alec Tiranti, London, 1956 (or Thames and Hudson, London, 1970)

Otto, Frei, *Tensile Structures*, M.I.T. Press, London, 1967

Salvadori, Mario, in collaboration with Robert Heller, *Structure in Architecture*, Prentice-Hall Inc., Eaglewood Cliffs, New Jersey, 1963

Siegel, Curt, *Structure and Form in Modern Architecture*, trans. Thomas E. Burton, Crosby Lockwood and Son Ltd., London, 1962

Stern, Robert, *New Directions in American Architecture*, Studio Vista, London, 1969

Torroja, Eduardo, *Philosophy of Structures*, English version by J. J. Polivka and Milos Polivka, University of California Press, Berkeley and Los Angeles, 1958

II   In addition the following may be found useful to provide a general background:

Allsop, Bruce, *The Study of Architectural History*, Studio Vista, London, 1970

Fletcher, Sir Banister, *A History of Architecture on the Comparative Method*, 17th edn., Athlone Press, University of London, 1961
> An old-timer, but still useful, especially for illustrations from all periods and places.

Fleming, Honour, Pevsner: *Penguin Dictionary of Architecture*, 2nd edn., Penguin Books, London, 1972
> Good ready reference.

Giedion, Sigfried, *Space, Time and Architecture*, Harvard University Press, Cambridge, Mass., 1943
> No longer new, but a dynamic approach to history.

The Great Ages of World Architecture, Studio Vista, London
> Excellent short guides to period styles and important examples.

The Pelican History of Art, ed. Nikolaus Pevsner, Penguin Books, London
> The best current volume by volume history of art and architecture.

> See especially the following:

Summerson, John, *Architecture in Britain 1530 to 1830*, 1953

Lawrence, A. W., *Greek Architecture*, 1957

Ward-Perkins, J. B., and Boethius, Axel, *Etruscan and Roman Architecture*, 1970

Frankl, Paul, *Gothic Architecture*, 1962

Notes

INTRODUCTION: IN PRAISE OF PRECEDENCE

1. Vitruvius, *The Ten Books on Architecture*, trans. Morris Hicky Morgan, Dover Publications, New York, 1960, Bk. 1, Ch. III, p. 17 ('durability, convenience and beauty').
2. *De Architectura Libri Decem*, evidently written in the reign of Augustus Caesar (Octavian) about 24 B.C.
3. Sir William Chambers, *A Treatise on Civil Architecture*, London, MDCCLIX, Preface p. iii.

I THE ART OF BUILDING

1. David Piper, *The Companion Guide to London*, Collins, 1964, p. 213.
2. Any illustrated reference to this group will indicate this, see, e.g. H. L. C. Jaffé, *de Stijl/1917–1931*, Alec Tiranti, 1956.
3. Bruno Zevi, *Architecture as Space*, Horizon Press, N.Y. 1957.
4. Vitruvius, *The Ten Books on Architecture*, trans. Morris Hicky Morgan, Dover Publications, New York, 1960, Bk. I, Ch. I.
5. Ibid., Bk. I, Ch. III.
6. Leone Battista Alberti, *Ten Books on Architecture*, trans. Leoni, Alec Tiranti, 1955, Bk. IX, Ch. X.
7. E.g. in a letter to a client recorded in his office notebook Add. 41133 p. 51 in the British Museum.
8. Vitruvius, op. cit., Bk. I, Ch. II.
9. Colen Campbell believed it was by Inigo Jones. John Summerson thinks it may have been designed by Nicholas Stone. See his *Architecture in Britain 1530 to 1830* in the Pelican History of Art Series, Penguin Books, 1953, p. 102.
10. In *Georgian London*, Pleiades Books, 1945.
11. Summerson, *Architecture in Britain*, p. 44.
12. Ibid., p. 35. Built between 1590 and 1597.
13. Although Summerson calls it a house 'of great and romantic beauty', ibid., p. 35.
14. Nikolaus Pevsner has written of this Elizabethan 'Mannerism', 'Double Profile', *Arch. Review*, March 1950, pp. 147–54.
15. By Robert Byron in *The Appreciation of Architecture*, Wishart and Co., 1932, p. 60.
16. Cf. Vernon Lee, *The Beautiful*, Cambridge University Press, 1913.
17. As pointed out by Elizabeth Mock, *The Architecture of Bridges*, Museum of Modern Art, New York, 1949.
18. M. S. Gregory, *History and Development of Engineering*, Longman, 1971, p. 16.
19. Ibid., p. 20.
20. Sigfried Giedion, *Space, Time and Architecture*, Harvard University Press, 4th edn., 1962, p. 488.
21. Mock, op. cit.
22. Cf. Peter Collins, *Changing Ideals in Modern Architecture 1750–1950*, Faber and Faber, first published 1965. 1971 edn., p. 187.
23. Ibid., p. 191. Fergusson was the author of *A History of Architecture in All Countries*, first published in 1893, and the *History of the Modern Styles of Architecture* which appeared in 1891.

24. Mock, op. cit., p. 7.
25. Gregory, op. cit., p. 55.
26. Referred to by Pevsner in *Studies in Art, Architecture and Design, Vol. II: Victorian and After*, Thames and Hudson, 1968, p. 39.
27. See Reyner Banham, *Theory and Design in the First Machine Age*, The Architectural Press, 1962, p. 252. Banham himself refers to the Orly hangars as 'Heroic but hardly architecture' in his *Guide to Modern Architecture*, The Architectural Press, 1962, p. 38.
28. Pier Luigi Nervi, *Aesthetics and Technology in Building*, trans. Robert Einardi, Harvard University Press, 1966, preface.

II THE CAVE AND THE CRYSTAL

1. See also Heather Martienssen, 'The Nature of Baroque: one: the Architecture of Excavation', *South African Architectural Record*, August 1950, pp. 176–82.
2. Cf. Zevi's attitude to space (op. cit.), and also S. E. Rasmussen, *Experiencing Architecture*, Chapman and Hall, 1959, pp. 48–50.
3. See also Rex Martienssen, *The Idea of Space in Greek Architecture*, Witwatersrand University Press, Johannesburg, 1956.
4. P. A. Michelis, *An Aesthetic Approach to Byzantine Art*, Batsford, 1955.
5. As developed by Buckminster Fuller.
6. See Ulrich Conrads, *Programmes and Manifestos on 20th-century Architecture*, Lund Humphries, 1970, p. 25.
7. *Architecture as Space*, trans. Milton Grendel, Horizon Press, New York, 1957, p. 143.
8. Quoted by Conrads, op. cit., p. 164.
9. See, for example, Peter Oliver, ed., *Shelter and Society*, The Cresset Press, Design Yearbook Ltd., 1969.
10. In *The Palaces of Crete*, Princeton University Press, 1962.
11. Moshe Safdie, *Beyond Habitat*, M.I.T. Press, Cambridge, Mass., 1970, p. 17.
12. In *Gothic Architecture*, The Pelican History of Art, Penguin Books, 1962, p. 39.
13. Illustrated in Frei Otto, *Spannweiten*, Verlag Ullstein, Berlin, 1965, p. 119.
14. Paul Heyer, *Architects on Architecture*, Walker and Co., New York, 1966, pp. 392 f.
15. Ibid., pp. 386 f.
16. Ibid., pp. 374 f.
17. All to be found in the *Encyclopaedia of Modern Architecture*, ed. Gerd Hatje, Thames and Hudson, 1963.
18. Ibid., p. 268.
19. See Maurice Besset, *Who was Le Corbusier?*, Skira, Geneva, c. 1968, p. 24.
20. Loc. cit.
21. Besset, op. cit., p. 41.
22. Other random examples are Johansen's Embassy at Dublin (1964), Breuer's I.B.M. Research Centre at La Gaude in the south of France, and the Carlton Centre in Johannesburg by Skidmore, Owings, and Merrill. See Heyer, op. cit., p. 377.
23. See Mock, op. cit., for a convincing apologia.
24. See also Mock, op. cit., p. 10.
25. *Encyclopaedia of Modern Architecture*, p. 268.
26. Alexander Cirici-Pellicer in the *Encyclopaedia of Modern Architecture*, p. 294.
27. *African Art and Leadership*, p. 145 ff.
28. J. Arnott Hamilton, *Byzantine Architecture and Decoration*, Batsford, 1956, p. 71.
29. By Deitrick and Nowicki, *Encyclopaedia of Modern Architecture*, p. 278.
30. Kenzo Tange, *Architecture and Urban Design 1946–1969*, Artemis, Zurich, 1970, p. 204.
31. In the *Companion Guide to Rome*, Collins, 1965, p. 19.

III THE PLAN AS THE GENERATOR

1. R. G. Collingwood, *The Principles of Art*, Oxford, 1938, Ch. VII esp. p. 125.
2. See his *Art*, Bodley Head, 1934.
3. In *Towards a new Architecture*.
4. Zevi, op. cit., p. 46.
5. S. E. Rasmussen, in *Experiencing Architecture* (1959) discusses this.
6. According to A. W. Lawrence, *Greek Architecture*, Pelican History of Art, Penguin Books, 1957, p. 248.
7. Though Ward-Perkins refers to this as the *Frigidarium*: J. B. Ward-Perkins and Axel Boethius, *Etruscan and Roman Architecture*, Pelican History of Art, Penguin Books, 1970, p. 272.
8. Hugh Plommer, *Ancient and Classical Architecture* (*Simpson's History of Architectural Development*, Vol. I), 1956, p. 341 now shows us that these were 'hot' rooms.
9. Cf. Ward-Perkins, op. cit., p. 272.
10. For example by older writers like Simpson.
11. Although Ward-Perkins has recently told us that there was in fact no earlier building (op. cit., p. 256).
12. Summerson, op. cit., p. 130.

IV CONCLUSION

1. Reyner Banham, *A Guide to Modern Architecture*, The Arch. Press, 1953, p. 152.

Index

Figures in bold type refer to pages on which illustrations occur